The Cyber Conundrum

The Cyber Conundrum

How Do We Fix Cybersecurity?

Peter K. Chronis

Printed in the United States of America

ISBN-13: 9781548860073
ISBN-10: 1548860077
Library of Congress Control Number: 2017918347
CreateSpace Independent Publishing Platform
North Charleston, South Carolina

To my husband, Michael, who has encouraged me to think differently and believe in the impossible.

Contents

Hope lies in dreams, in imagination, and in the courage of those who dare to make dreams into reality.

—Jonas Salk

A rising tide lifts all boats.

—President John F. Kennedy

Preface

Let me start by saying that this book is both enhanced and constrained by my own experiences managing IT and business risk over the last twenty years. I have spent most of my career as a cybersecurity professional on the frontlines of the war against hackers. I have led teams that have stopped more than $100 million in online fraud and blocked more than 750 billion cybersecurity attacks. Despite those results, I never felt like the work I was doing was enough. I was managing cybersecurity problems, not solving them. But that's the nature of today's cybersecurity warriors: no matter how good you are, there's always another attack around the corner or the mother of all security issues waiting in the shadows, ready to spread havoc.

Cybersecurity professionals are a lot like emergency-room doctors. Cybersecurity pros are focused on triaging and containing the impact of security incidents. Doctors are focused on ensuring patients are stabilized and treated. Neither cybersecurity pros nor ER doctors have much of an impact on the broader issues that drive incidents (e.g., bugs in commercial software or lack of a national cybersecurity strategy) or ER patient visits (e.g., alcohol consumption, opioid addiction, or lack of preventive care). By their very nature, they are both tacticians—not strategists. What I'm proposing in this book is a radical shift in national cybersecurity strategy, not an incremental shift in tactics.

I certainly don't have all the answers, but one thing I have learned over the years is that our current approach for addressing cybersecurity challenges is not working, and it is not sustainable.

Our adversaries always seem to be one step ahead of us. So the big conundrum is what we have to do to regain the upper hand. How can we win? Are we willing to change?

I believe there is hope for solving the cybersecurity conundrum if we let history be our guide. We can look for inspiration from other innovators who have faced problems bigger than the solutions available to solve them. Let's learn from these innovators' hard lessons and adapt those lessons in a way that helps us get beyond the current state of ineffective cybersecurity.

I believe radical change is needed before we can take back the advantage from our adversaries. I hope to inspire the debate for radical change in the cybersecurity community through this book or, if nothing else, to help myself more clearly articulate the problems as I see them.

Introduction

Postwar America in 1948 was a promising place. World War II was over, hundreds of thousands of servicemen returned home, and the prospects for American supremacy seemed assured. The dark clouds that hovered over America's collective psyche, colored by both the Great Depression and the world's deadliest war, were fading. For the first time in history, America was leading the world in scientific research, and pent-up demand for consumer goods drove a new wave of prosperity, ushering in capitalism's Golden Age.[1, 2]

Two key innovations that would eventually change the world as we know it were born during the postwar boom. The transistor, invented in late 1947, has been called one of history's most important innovations.[3] In essence, the transistor—the key component of all microprocessors, the brain of today's modern computers, mobile phones, and smart devices—influences the way we work, live, and play.

The second innovation, found in an article titled "The Mathematical Theory of Communications," was proposed by thirty-three-year-old electrical engineer and mathematician Claude Shannon and published in the Bell Systems Technical Journal.[4] Shannon was an innovator and his early research became the foundation for digital circuit design used in every modern computer today.[5] In "Theory of Communications" Shannon laid out the basic constructs used in communications technology that powers our digital world today.

Shannon's time as a cryptographer during World War II was influenced by Dutch linguist and cryptographer Auguste Kerchkoff, whose Kerchkoff's Principle sets the security standard all modern cryptographic systems use today.[6] Shannon wasn't just a revolutionary thinker; he was also a staunch realist. He adapted Kerchkoff's Principle into his own design philosophy, suggesting that we should "design [technical] systems under the assumption that the enemy will immediately gain full familiarity with them."[7] While Shannon was primarily referring to cryptographic systems, he was also foreshadowing a new reality within the digital and connected world he helped create—a world where defective software, hardware, and networks would be exploited by a new generation of curious technophiles, criminals, spies, misfits, and soldiers we now refer to as hackers.

No one could predict the rapid technical revolution that followed the innovations of the late 1940s, including the development of the personal computer, the Internet, mobile phones, and the software revolution. All of those technological advances evolved so rapidly and converged so quickly that it astounded those of us who were around to witness them.

Along the way, Shannon's dire warning never found a place, as tech companies fought for technical supremacy and market share in this rapidly evolving landscape. Today, software and hardware defects are released into the world by the thousands each year in commercial software and serve as fodder for modern hackers.

But what does this mean to a modern society increasingly reliant on Internet-enabled commerce, mobile communication, social media, nonstop news, cheap energy, and ubiquitous access to information? It means the underlying technology fueling modern conveniences, our economy, and our general way of life is flawed and vulnerable. Nearly every area of the global economy runs on flawed software and hardware designed and produced without Shannon's maxim in mind. Why? Few foresaw how our modern society would come to rely on technology and how exposed we might be.

We live in a time when many believe hacking is an unstoppable phenomenon, and many don't explore the role modern technologists play in unwittingly helping hackers. Buggy software leaves behind holes hackers can use to take over computers, penetrate networks, and gain access to sensitive data.

The vast majority of our citizens are concerned about identity theft and cybersecurity, but few take accountability for their own digital hygiene. We barely flinch when we hear news about how the NSA uses hacking tools to spy on adversaries, learn of new hacks involving millions of stolen passwords, or learn of companies crippled by smoking-hole attacks left behind by hackers who have scores to settle. Smoking-hole attacks focus on causing extreme disruption, with the sole purpose of interrupting an organization's or industry's ability to operate.

What is the cyber conundrum? In this book, we'll explore why we're losing the battle against hackers, consider why this battle is important to all of us, and explore some of the challenges we face when trying to address the major realities that hackers take advantage of on a daily basis. Fixing cybersecurity is a complex challenge, but the true conundrum lies in our ability to convince cybersecurity and technology stakeholders that change is truly needed before it is too late.

We'll look for inspiration by investigating how other complex challenges were solved in the past—especially where those challenges required a change in public opinion or a realignment of national priorities. In the end, I'll propose a series of fundamental changes in how we should approach cybersecurity and make the case for why change is needed now.

Part 1: What's Wrong with Cybersecurity?

I

Losing the War

For more than twenty years, technologists have been warning about cybersecurity vulnerabilities and weaknesses. One of the earliest advocates for cybersecurity reform was a group of hackers from Boston named L0ft. L0ft started as a collective, a place for like-minded technophiles to collaborate. Like many technophiles, they explored technology to see how it worked. Along the way, they found multiple security holes that many vendors refused to fix. As L0ft members testified, companies warned about security flaws in their products "seemed unresponsive to complaints [made] through formal channels."[8]

Paul Nash, a member of L0ft who went by the hacker pseudonym Silicosis, described his experience with the rapid pace of software development and lack of security by saying the software industry seemed to think, "[G]et it up, get it running as fast as we can. Let's make some money...we'll fix it later."[9]

Members of L0ft, using the aliases No, Space Rogue, Kingpin, and Mudge, testified before the Senate in May 1998.[10] They told senators that the "fix it later" mentality left computers, networks, and the Internet insecure and vulnerable to attack. The threat was so severe that Senator Fred Thompson believed immediate action was required to address this issue before things got out of hand.[11] The result was one of the biggest missed opportunities of the modern era. Little money is spent today on addressing the root cause of security problems that plague cybersecurity. A recent Reuters article found the federal government is doing little to defend American companies; rather, "across the federal government, about 90 percent of all spending on cyber programs is dedicated to offensive efforts, including penetrating the computer systems of adversaries, listening to communications and developing the means to disable or degrade infrastructure."[12]

This "fix it later" mentality within the software industry introduces risk to all consumers, businesses, and governments that use their commercial software. Fixing often is done via software updates or "patches" provided by the vendor that can be installed on computers running the flawed software version.

Commercial software vendors such as Microsoft, Google, and Apple release hundreds of security patches each year. Many must be installed manually or must be tested by organizations before installation, creating a difficult challenge for companies constrained by already-tight budgets. Microsoft issues security patches monthly on "Patch Tuesday." Oracle issues patches quarterly. But patches do not always keep up to date with vulnerabilities as they are discovered. In a recent software patch update, Oracle released a fix for a five-year-old bug in its Java open-source software that runs on billions of devices globally.[13]

Fast-forward to today. Cybercrime damage is estimated to cost $3 trillion a year and is expected to double by 2021.[14] Nearly one-third of American companies were victims of cybercrime.[15] Nearly four billion customer records were stolen in 2016 alone.[16] It is nearly impossible to find a positive statistic on the state of cybersecurity today.

Superhacks began hitting the news in 2013. Four of the five largest breaches in history occurred in 2013 and 2014.[17] Yahoo, Target, Home Depot, eBay, Adobe, and JP Morgan all announced breaches during 2013 and 2014, totaling more than 1.8 billion customer records.[18] Then 2014 was capped by one of the most destructive attacks ever witnessed, when the entire computer network of Sony Pictures was hacked in an elaborate cyber-ransom operation that made headlines across the globe.

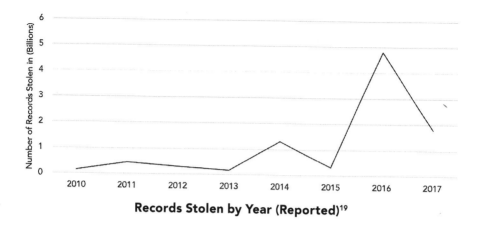

Records Stolen by Year (Reported)[19]

Things went from bad to worse between 2015 and 2016. The total number of data breaches reported in the United States jumped 40 percent between those two years.[20] Breaches at Anthem and the US Office of Personnel Management conducted by nation-state hackers dominated the news.

A recent Pew Research Center survey found half of Americans feel that their personal information is less safe than it was five years ago.[21] It is easy to see why. That same study found 64 percent of respondents had been victims of a major data breach.

If the government isn't doing enough to protect us from cybersecurity threats, are consumers doing a better job protecting themselves? The Pew Research Center recently performed a survey of Americans to see if all these breach reports were changing behaviors online. While the report found consumers lacked confidence that companies could protect their personal information, consumers were not altering their behaviors and habits.[22] The study found the following:

- 41 percent of online adults have shared the password to one of their online accounts with a friend or family member.
- 39 percent say they use the same or very similar passwords for many of their online accounts.
- 25 percent admit they often use insecure passwords because they are easier to remember.

- 28 percent of smartphone owners report that they do not use a screen lock or other security features in order to protect their phone.
- 10 percent never install updates to their smartphone's apps or operating system.

These lax practices make it easier for criminals and hackers to gain access to customer online banking, e-mail, device backups, and other sensitive information. It is hard to fault consumers for poor password security. Many consumers have between two and three dozen online identities to manage.[23] Memorizing complex, unique passwords for each of those sites is way too complicated for anyone without a photographic memory.

So how are America's businesses doing protecting themselves from cyber threats? According to consulting firm PWC's 2017 Global Economic Crime Survey, cybercrime is the second costliest economic crime facing companies.[23] Further, a recent New York Stock Exchange survey found that two-thirds of corporate boards of directors did not believe their companies were prepared to address cybersecurity risk.[25]

Cybercrime is costing companies big money. Yahoo shareholders were forced to reduce their company's sale price by $350 million after Verizon became aware of Yahoo's massive data breach. Yahoo executives also forfeited millions in bonuses or were fired as a result of the breach.[26, 27] Target's and Equifax's massive breaches were enough to cause their CEOs to resign.[28]

Where risk is believed to be high, spending follows. Corporate cybersecurity spending is expected to more than double between 2015 and 2020.[29] Time will tell if this new emphasis on cybersecurity will help reverse the tide of disruptive attacks.

Worse than attacks against companies, cybersecurity threats may undermine the very institutions that modern democracies rely on across the globe. Fake news, election-system hacking, and meddling dominated the 2016 US presidential election. There is no ambiguity as to whether Russia is using cyber information operations to spread "fake news and propaganda, and they also used online amplifiers to spread the information to as many people as possible," according to Bill Priestap, the FBI's head of counterintelligence.[30] Intelligence officials warned evidence has come to light that shows the orders to conduct the operation came from Russian president Vladimir Putin himself.[31]

It is difficult to measure the scope and impact of Russia's information operations, but signs point out that it has been massive. Evidence indicates that ads and fake news on platforms such as Facebook and Twitter were seen by hundreds of millions during the course of the election.[32] The electoral college was decided by fewer than 110,000 votes, making any interference of the scale witnessed in the election suspect of influencing the outcome.[33]

It is worth considering how fake news is used to influence public opinion and makes its way into mainstream reporting. Fake news is designed to manipulate public opinion to achieve a geopolitical outcome. Its occurrences are intentional and conducted by governments and nonstate actors alike.

126 MILLION
Number of individuals who viewed Russian Facebook Ads during the US election

288 MILLION
Number of views on Twitter of posts from Russian government sponsored accounts

Electoral votes needed for a Clinton win: 38

Key States that Could Have Changed the Outcome

	Votes	Electors	Margin
Wisconsin:	27K	10	.8%
Pennsylvania:*	68K	20	.7%
Michigan:	11K	16	.2%
Total:	107K	46	

* Evidence of Russian targeted campaigns to voters

Did Russian Ads Sway the Election?[34, 35]

Facebook's white paper on fake news titled "Information Operations and Facebook"[36] identified three core elements of information operations, including:

- Disinformation: The process of creating fake news focused on influencing public opinion. Disinformation is often bent in a way to influence certain key demographic groups.
- Fake News: Stories that appear to be true but contain inaccurate information designed to appeal to fringe groups or support a specific methodology.
- Fake Amplifiers: Thousands of fake social media accounts generated to create scale in distributing false news. These sites amplify the original fake news story, which tricks social media platforms into including those articles in news feeds belonging to real people. Those folks help spread the fake news to other real users.

A *New York Times* exposé explored the fake-news ecosystem and showed how difficult it is to trace fake news back to its original source.[37] The exposé investigated a military incident from 2014 that was resurrected three years later in a fake news story and later reported by the mainstream media. The navy reported the incident when a Russian warplane buzzed a US warship in the Black Sea. The fake news report indicated the flyover tested a new Russian technology that completely disabled the ship's computer systems, rendering the ship inoperable. The story spread so quickly that it made its way to Russian TV and then to legitimate, respected Western media sources.

As both the *New York Times* and Facebook study report, there are several evident phases of fake news:

1. **Parody:** News starts out as a fake story on a website designed to look like a real news site.

2. **Amplification:** The fake news story is distributed by thousands of fake accounts on social media that are followed or liked by others.

3. **Laundering:** The story gains momentum on social media and gains credibility when traditional news sources report on it indirectly with language such as "Russian TV is reporting..."

4. **Legitimizing:** Disinformation is further legitimized when it is reported by a traditional media outlet and is considered fact.

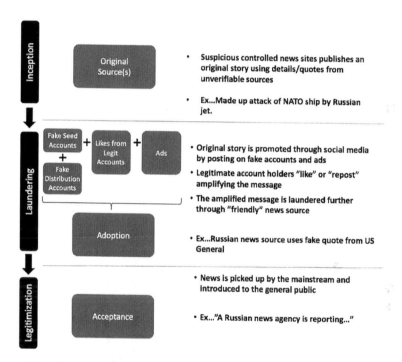

Fake News: Social Media Disinformation Campaign Phases

Russian fake news sites such as RT and Sputnik mix questionable content with legitimate news stories, making it difficult to distinguish fact from fiction.[38]

Learning hard lessons from the fallout from the US elections, Facebook teamed up with local media groups to identify and eliminate fake news distributed on the social media site. Facebook reportedly shuttered thirty thousand fake accounts in the run-up to the French election in 2017 as EU proponent Emanuel Macron faced off against Francophile Marine Le Pen.[39]

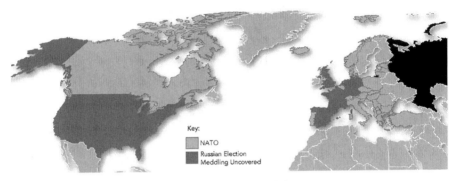

Russian Election Meddling

From our brief analysis, it is clear that cybersecurity challenges are getting costlier and more impactful and are putting critical areas of our economy and society in jeopardy. Solving complex cybersecurity challenges is not within our immediate grasp. But what does success look like? Would we know good cybersecurity if we saw it?

Defining cybersecurity success has subjective and objective measures. Zero breaches, no downtime, and meeting patch service-level objectives are all measures that might describe how your company is performing. There are a number of subjective measures worth considering: Are we safe online? Can we trust technology? Will IT systems work when we need them to?

It is clear that if solving cybersecurity challenges were easy, it would have been done already. It is worth exploring the complex factors that make solving cybersecurity challenges so difficult.

II

Why Is Cybersecurity So Hard?

Michael Daniel, former special assistant to the president and cybersecurity coordinator at the White House, believes the very nature of cybersecurity threats is different from other security challenges. Technology erases boundaries and brings adversaries within striking distance of critical assets. He highlights the challenge: "With distances greatly reduced, threats can literally come from anywhere and from any actor."[40]

Another fact is that good cybersecurity is hard because it is complex. The relationship among threat-actor motivations, threats, and technology is a complicated web. When we create a visual problem model to identify the relationships among these three variable categories, we find a complex web, making comprehensive solutions elusive.

Motivation		Threats		Technologies	
financial	political	malware	botnets	software	networks
altruistic	deception	vulnerabilities	DDoS	computers	Internet of things
espionage	disruption	worms	social engineering	mobile devices	social media
influence		exploits	phishing	email	internet
		ID theft		cloud	satellites
				quantum computing	artificial intelligence

Simplified Cybersecurity Problem Model

The complexity of the problem, the high stakes, and the rapid evolution of the threat mean half measures will not be effective.

Hackers depend on human error to help propel most of their activities. They rely on social-engineering techniques to trick users into clicking on links in e-mails through phishing. To conduct more sophisticated hacking, they rely on bugs in commercial software left behind by software developers. These bugs, also called vulnerabilities, can be used by hackers to manipulate software to do things it is not supposed to do.

Many consider phone phreaking to be the earliest form of hacking. Starting in the 1950s, Phreakers used toy whistles to play special tones in the mouthpiece of phones to trick automated telephone switching systems into allowing free long-distance calls.[40] Imagine the creativity and effort it must have taken to reverse-engineer switching systems to learn how they work and how to circumvent them.

But how does software hacking work? Let's consider another rebel from the 1950s, Arthur Fonzarelli. Sure, Fonzie was legendarily cool, but he wasn't magic. Fonzie knew how to hack his way through life. With one jab on the jukebox, he could force it to play music without depositing any coins. We think his coolness made the jukebox go; the fictional reality is that he knew how to exploit a vulnerability in its design to make it behave in an unintended way.

Hacking software is just like phone phreaking and Fonzie's jukebox trick—hackers exploit design flaws, weaknesses, and/or human error.

Adding to the challenge, operating-system software used to run computers has become more complex over the last ten years. The code base behind Windows and Linux operating systems are ten times larger today than they were ten years ago.[42] So how good has the commercial software industry been at improving security while the complexity of its software increases? It is easy to see there is plenty of progress to be made.

To explore this point further, let's look at the total number of software vulnerabilities reported in commercial software.

Commercial software is the software that runs your laptop, smartphone, or tablet—it runs your spreadsheets, documents, photos, music playlists, and much more. Software packages from Google, Microsoft, Oracle, and Apple run on more devices than any other. Other types of commercial software include productivity software (e.g., Microsoft Word), database software that stores large amounts of data (e.g., Oracle), e-mail services (e.g., Gmail and Yahoo), and industrial software (e.g., Siemens).

Known software bugs, called vulnerabilities, identified in commercial software are recorded in the National Vulnerability Database (NVD), which is maintained by the National Institute of Standards and Technology (NIST). Looking at data from the NVD from the last ten years, security professionals identified an average of approximately six thousand security vulnerabilities in commercial software each year.[43]

Vulnerability reports remained consistent for seven of the last ten years, but an interesting trend emerged in 2017: the total vulnerabilities discovered in commercial software reported doubled from 2016.

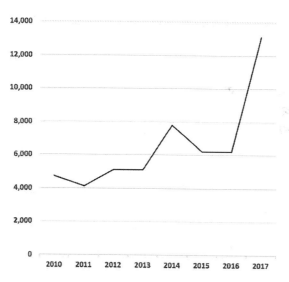

NIST: Commercial Software Vulnerabilities 2010–2017[44]

There are no outliers in the data (operating system, vendor, and so on). There aren't new detection techniques, and there's no evidence more researchers are now contributing to the data. The trend shows that the commercial software industry is not getting better at finding code bugs before software is released to the public. These new vulnerabilities give hackers more ways to attack than ever before.

It is not that companies aren't trying. Microsoft spends more than a billion dollars a year on security,[45] and much of that goes toward protecting its source code intellectual property and testing its own software for bugs. Across all industries, companies will soon spend more than $100 billion collectively each year to protect their employees, networks, data, and intellectual property.[46] That means company cybersecurity spending is nearly one-tenth of what the world spends on national defense.[47] You would expect that an enormous sum like that might be enough to thwart hackers. The truth is, it is barely making a dent.

Software vulnerability-detection techniques do not identify all the potential ways hackers can exploit software. Hackers rely on software bugs, poor software/hardware configuration, and human error to hack. If they can find the right bug, they might be able to hack their way onto a computer or server without logging on, steal data from a database, place software on a server, and/or execute software commands without anyone knowing.

Just knowing about the existence of a software bug is usually not enough. Hackers must weaponize the vulnerability to take full advantage of it. Software programs called exploits use special techniques to take advantage of software vulnerabilities and weaponize them. Exploits can be run by hand by hackers, run automatically, or be delivered via malware embedded in websites, programs, or e-mails.

Nearly all exploits rely on a few dozen techniques to exploit bugs in commercial software such as an operating system or a spreadsheet program. Some target specific commercial software, such as industrial control systems used in factories or power plants.

Not all vulnerabilities are reported and fixed. Many discovered by criminals and spies are kept secret. These secret vulnerabilities are called zero-day vulnerabilities and usually are used to conduct sophisticated hacking and espionage.

The National Security Agency (NSA) is the United States' premier cyber-spying agency. Its 2013 budget was reported to be around $10 billion.[48] The NSA spends billions a year looking for zero-day vulnerabilities, weaponizing them, and conducting offensive operations and espionage. That's good when those tools stay secret. It is bad when these zero-day vulnerabilities don't stay secret or are stolen or when someone else discovers them too.

The WannaCry malware outbreak in 2017 was a great example of what happens when these secret vulnerabilities make their way to the outside world. WannaCry relied on a previously unknown vulnerability stolen from the NSA and weaponized and released by hackers. WannaCry spread globally, infecting tens of thousands of computers. The WannaCry exploit wasn't sophisticated, and its spread was thwarted by a clever researcher. But the malware infection highlights how, in just a few weeks, a cyber pandemic can spread globally where most companies are ill prepared to defend themselves.

Sony was not the first targeted smoking-hole attack—Saudi Aramco and attacks against a number of South Korean public- and private-sector entities were the earliest ones.

At Aramco, employees came in one morning to find that their computer hard drives had been erased. Iran was given credit for this attack—targeting a Saudi state-owned enterprise. Meanwhile, North Korea was tied to a series of crippling attacks that caused massive business disruption in South Korea. Neither caused long-term disruption, but they did usher in a new era of disruptive attacks.

It is easy to see how Sony became the event that awakened the world to the potential damage a cyberattack can cause. Long believed unworthy of the focus that banks, defense contractors, and research labs received from hackers, media companies had something some hackers found threatening or valuable: reach and influence.

Imagine an era where geopolitical conflicts start when adversaries attack non-military targets first like power grids, financial institutions and media outlets. In this likely scenario, our traditional media outlets are silenced by cyberattacks, and fake news outlets are amplified causing mass disruption and confusion. Other nonmilitary targets are attacked in a relentless onslaught—and the beginnings of a siege mentality start to grip the general public. That's the promise of a new type of warfare—one that is widespread, relentless, and very damaging to nonmilitary targets. Since many of us use the same commercial software to run our data centers, desktops, or laptops, attackers can weaponize one or two vulnerabilities and unleash them in the hopes of causing worldwide disruption.

While cybersecurity is evolving and spending is up in the public and private sectors, the cybersecurity community's collective defenses are unable to keep up with this evolving threat. Widespread smoking-hole attacks have taught us that protecting the private sector from cyberattacks should be a national security imperative. But how do we respond to the threat at scale when nearly all the infrastructure at risk is unregulated and in the hands of the private sector? What do we do when our government's cybersecurity priorities are focused not on defensive initiatives but on offensive operations?

The reality is that better firewalls or malware-detection technologies aren't enough to address sophisticated threats. While firewalls, malware detection, and other security technologies in general have dramatically improved over the last few years they are not stemming the tide of breaches and disruptive attacks. Instead, breaches and disruptive attacks are on the rise.

We need fresh thinking in the way we protect ourselves against the massive threat of cyberattacks. Incremental prevention and detection improvements will not help us avoid cybersecurity peril in the future. We don't need tactical solutions; we need a comprehensive national strategy that will help us address the fundamentals driving cyber insecurity.

III

Making the Case for Change

The world is a much healthier place than it ever has been. Extreme poverty as a percentage of the total population is down.[49] More people have access to clean water and health care than ever before.[50, 51] The average lifespan here in the United States has grown by about twenty years per person in the last one hundred years.[52] Despite what we hear nearly every day in the news, it is easy to argue that we live in a golden age of prosperity and longevity unseen in human history.

There are still plenty of unsolved challenges that put our collective longevity and prosperity in jeopardy. Global warming, homelessness, poverty, and economic disparity are still challenges our society has yet to solve. Many of those challenges don't immediately affect the majority of Americans and therefore don't get the attention and focus they need. Cybersecurity challenges also put American prosperity at risk if we fail to educate citizens and lawmakers of the need to address cyber risk as a national security and economic priority. Prolonged cybersecurity attacks could devastate our economy and threaten the average American's way of life.

Case in point: Meet Henrietta Stone. She's not a real person; I've made her up to help illustrate a point. She and her husband,

Clyde, earn the average household income of about $66,000 a year after taxes.[53] They live in an affordable community and own their own home, where they live with their two children. Seventy-five percent of their income has been gobbled up by housing, transportation, food, and health care. The hardest economic reality for the Stone family is that despite all their hard work, their expenses keep going up while income stays flat.[54] It feels harder and harder for the Stones to make ends meet. This is not surprising—the latest studies indicate that work and financial issues are two of the top three sources of worry for adults in America.[55] It is no wonder that nearly half of Americans live paycheck to paycheck.[56] Wages have not been keeping up with inflation for decades.

> Average annual growth in nonfarm business sector real compensation per hour, which includes wages, salaries and benefits paid to workers, registered 1.4 percent from 1956 to 2016, and 1.5 percent from 1956 to 2006. However, from 2007 to 2016—covering the recession and subsequent recovery-expansion period—real compensation per hour growth averaged only 0.6 percent. And since the start of the recovery in mid-2009, again, growth has averaged a woeful 0.6 percent.[57]

The vast majority of Americans live like the Stones—perilously close to the economic edge. As the statistics above point out, they're less prosperous. Economic stability is absolutely essential to survival. The chart below captures the average American household's expense-to-income ratio during the Great Recession. Wages stagnated as expenses climbed, adding immense pressure to those already on the economic edge.

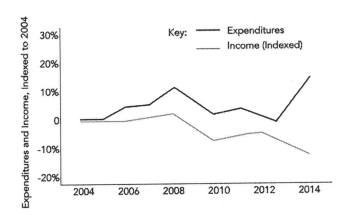

American Household Income-to-Expense Ratio[86]

We know technology plays an important part in American prosperity. Technology is everywhere we look today: in our cars, our phones, and our homes. It surrounds us wherever we go. Nearly every area of our economy is dependent on commercial off-the-shelf software and hardware. For example, banks, telecommunications companies, first responders, and hospitals are all dependent on commercial technology to function. The question is, what would happen to society and the economy if they were under persistent cyberattack?

To make matters more complex, our economy and society are in the middle of three massive technical revolutions that are converging at light speed. Revolutions in digital communications technology, big-data analytics, and artificial intelligence are currently underway. We're barely starting to grasp how breakthroughs in each of these areas will fuel the global economy. Experts believe they will drive more than a trillion dollars of economic benefit in the next few years.[59] Our future economic growth is intertwined with technology like never before.

Many war planners believe cyber warfare is here to stay and can be used to disrupt an adversary's economy, society, and ability to conduct war.[60] Is this just fantasy and paranoia, or is there actual evidence that persistent warfare is likely in the future? The truth is, that era is already upon us.

There is no better laboratory on Earth in which to look at the impacts of sustained cyber warfare on a modern society than in Ukraine. Since "little green men" invaded ethnic Russian enclaves in eastern Ukraine and the Crimea, the country has sustained relentless attacks in nearly every area of the economy. As *Wired* reports, "the [electricity] blackouts weren't just isolated attacks. They were part of a digital blitzkrieg that has pummeled Ukraine for the past three years—a sustained cyber assault unlike any the world has ever seen...wave after wave of intrusions have deleted data, destroyed computers, and in some cases paralyzed organizations' most basic functions."[61]

Many believe Russians are capable of more disruptive attacks and expect even more damage from future conflicts.[62] While many Ukrainians have not felt the burden of this persistent cyber warfare, many of Ukraine's companies have been thrown into chaos, and the economy is in shambles.

Gross domestic product (GDP) declined by nearly 15 percent during the three years of war with Russia.[63] No reliable figures are available to indicate the total impact of cyberattacks on the economy. It is clear that mass cyber disruption on the scale of Russia's Ukrainian campaign would have massive implications on our economy and society.

If we surmise that just a fraction of Ukraine's GDP decline was caused by massive cyberattacks and theoretically apply those to the US economy, the impacts could be severe. How do we evaluate the potential impact of a persistent cyberattack on the United States?

Let's begin by exploring Okun's Law, which tracks the relationship between GDP and unemployment. GDP is often used to measure the health of the economy because it is the measure of all goods and services produced by a country. Okun's Law is a well-respected economic principle that measures the impact of changes in GDP on employment. If GDP falls by 2 percent, unemployment increases by 1 percent.[64]

Using Okun's Law and recent stats from the US Bureau of Labor Statistics,[65] we can estimate that a 1 percent decline in US GDP could cost approximately half a million jobs, as businesses lay off workers to compensate for declining revenues.

Could persistent cyberattacks against American companies do that much economic damage? If you look at the business sectors targeted by cyberattacks in Ukraine regularly, those same sectors make up more than 30 percent of the United States' $18.6 trillion economy.[66] Persistent power outages, disruption of supply chains, and telecommunications and network outages like those experienced in Ukraine could be incredibly disruptive in our technology-driven economy. If hackers could disrupt at least 5 percent of our economy through persistent attacks over a long period of time, we'd see an economic impact where nearly 2.5 million people might lose their jobs.[67]

But how likely are these types of cyberattacks against American companies? Many experts believe they are very likely, and it is easy to see why: we have seen countless examples of how attacks against private companies have massive consequences.

A smoking-hole attack is the most severe type of cyber operation. As we discussed earlier, the most famous smoking-hole attack occurred at Sony and was repeatedly attributed to North Korea. Fueled by the release of a film that depicted the North Korean leader Kim Jong-un as weak and incompetent, one of the world's most isolated countries launched a cyberattack straight out of the pages of a spy novel.

Employees arriving at Sony Entertainment headquarters in Culver City, California, on the morning of Monday, November 24, were unable to access e-mail, open files, print checks, or perform any work requiring a computer. Instead, they were greeted by grotesque images of the decapitated head of the studio's CEO on their computer screens, part of an elaborate attack on the company's IT systems.[68] It was a disruption that lasted for many months.

The attack was the start of a long cyber operation focused on punishing Sony for making the film *The Interview*. The movie's launch was put on hold as fear swept the nation. A disinformation campaign sprung up circulating bomb threats against theaters that decided to show the movie. The film's actors went underground, and a media frenzy ensued. Many believed the studio caved to hacker demands; meanwhile, Sony was nowhere close to recovering from the attack.

The Sony attack was part of a new era of cyber attacks that just didn't steal data but also caused physical damage. These kinds of

> direct, negative impact on revenue is a new wrinkle in information security, and it should convince executives and boards of directors in all sectors that information security and risk management are fundamental requirements of a profitable business.[69]

The Sony attack helps illustrate this new era of physical smoking-hole attacks that can target industrial control systems—such as those used in manufacturing and utilities,[70] or those used to produce and distribute information to the public.[71] It is entirely likely that what is happening today in Ukraine could happen to the rest of the world—at scale.

We're truly in new territory. At no point in the last two generations has the United States been so vulnerable to disruption from a foreign threat. Despite the rhetoric of the Cold War, Russia did not have the capability to invade the United States and disrupt America's way of life without assuredly facing total obliteration.

The new reality is that cyber threats will disrupt our economy and our way of life in the future unless we change the way we protect government and private-sector infrastructure. That type of change needed is within our grasp—but not if we stick to the tools and practices we use today.

If we were well on our way to solving cybersecurity challenges, there would be evidence. The number of vulnerabilities in commercial software would decline, fewer breaches would be recorded, financial gains from cybercrimes would decline, and we'd hear less about cybercrime in the news. Unfortunately, none of these trends appear evident.

So despite huge increases in cybersecurity spending in the US public and private sectors, why do we not see more progress? I would argue that the reason for the lack of progress is that we are focusing on the wrong priorities. Incremental improvements will not address cybersecurity risk in a meaningful way. Progress requires a more significant approach because the problems are complex and will require innovation and discipline to solve.

We need fresh thinking and a new approach. We need to change the way we build software. We need to reduce the impact of human error in contributing to cyberattacks. We need to change government priorities to focus on defensive operations rather than offensive operations. Private companies must do more too, enhancing their own security and demanding better security in their supply chain.

In truth, we need a cybersecurity moonshot to align priorities and make real progress in addressing the root causes that make us so vulnerable today.

Part 2: Exploring Moonshots

IV

Solving Difficult Problems

Studies show 80 percent of the decisions humans make are based on emotion, while 20 percent are based on logic.[72] The motivation behind solving a complex problem can be emotional; however, the steps identified to address it must be fueled by methodical and logical thinking.

Moonshots are nothing more than a call to action to solve complex problems. The word *moonshot* came from America's quest to land a man on the moon, and the term continues to inspire today. Whether it is the cure for cancer, the desire to end poverty, or the quest to end homelessness, calls to action can drive positive outcomes that benefit society over the long term.

Researchers suggest "a successful moonshot requires a sufficient understanding of the basic science underlying a problem in question so that efforts can be focused on engineering a solution."[73]

Cancer researchers are severely hampered by what they do not know about the disease. But researchers, bolstered by past successful scientific endeavors, are confident that with enough research and time, they'll overcome the gaps and achieve success.

If we're truly going to succeed in creating a cybersecurity moonshot movement, we'll need a bit of inspiration and lessons taken from other successful complex endeavors. We'll need inspiration from innovators who took risks on endeavors too big to fail. It is worth exploring three key complex initiatives whose missions were not assured at their starts. In our search for inspiration that can help our journey, we'll explore sending humans to the moon, defeating fascism during World War II, and the eradication of polio in the United States. Solving those very different challenges involved complex solutions that did not exist when these efforts were initially started. So before we propose solutions in our moonshot journey, it's probably worth a quick study on how complex problems are solved and how moonshots are structured.

Let's start with common elements we noticed in our study of moonshots we'll explore in greater detail in later chapters. We noticed most moonshots began as a crisis or series of events that required some sort of collective, complex set of actions to resolve. The crisis and its resulting dialogue raise awareness of the problems and penalties, often resulting in a call to action. A call to action requires enlightened and/or motivated leaders who marshal resources, foster collaboration, and develop a strategy. Most complex problems require iterative, dynamic decision making throughout the execution phase as new facts become available or the problem evolves.

Moonshot Phases

Researchers at Purdue University suggest a methodical approach to problem solving that involves fact-finding and fact-reduction processes to help identify a model that evolves as facts shift and change.[74] Solutions may evolve as facts on the ground change, requiring dynamic decision making.

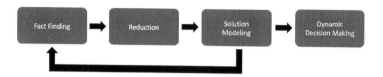

Purdue Problem-Solving Model

When we merge our moonshot and problem-solving models, we see a complex process we should consider following for our own initiative.

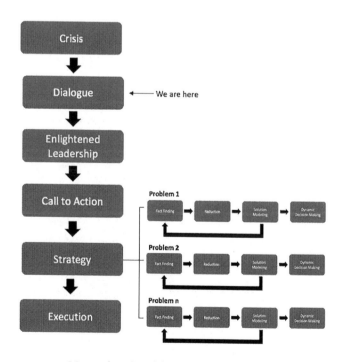

Moonshot/Problem-Solving Model

Ultimately, we need to change long-standing norms that are driving unproductive behavior if we want to solve the cyber conundrum. Norms "are rules of conduct that govern interactions among key groups."[75] Norms drive powerful forces that influence behavior in everyday life—influencing outcomes that affect our conundrum.

Norms drive both group and individual behavior. If we are successful, our moonshot will recognize and address norms at all levels.

We need to address norms driving unhealthy results in the software industry, among the general public, corporations and government to resolve our conundrum successfully. We'll explore how we address these norms in later chapters.

The most difficult elements in solving complex problems lie in building a solutions model that alters harmful norms. The first three chapters in this book will serve as our fact-finding exercise. The last four chapters will suggest problems that should be addressed in our moonshot that change the norms fueling our conundrum.

There will be no shortage of challenges addressing cybersecurity norms. We haven't figured out how to write bug-free software on a commercial scale, and we certainly don't know how to remove human error in the way technology is used or abused. It is also worth noting that while there has been much success in changing American policy priorities to address other challenges, doing so is a very complex and difficult process. While these issues may seem insurmountable, there is too much at stake to leave these problems unsolved. We don't have to look far to see how other similar insurmountable challenges were addressed. In the next few chapters, we'll explore other moonshots and look for inspiration and lessons we can apply to addressing cybersecurity challenges.

V

Getting a Man to the Moon

Science-fiction writers have played an important role in capturing the imagination of scientists and aspiring scientists alike. Author Eileen Gunn writes, "Sometimes it's the seemingly weird ideas that come true—thanks, in part, to science fiction's capacity to spark an imaginative fire in readers who have the technical knowledge to help realize its visions."[76]

Jules Verne continued a very long tradition among writers of using the moon to capture his readers' collective imagination. One hundred and three years before the first lunar orbit, Verne teased the very thoughts of traveling to the moon in his book *From the Earth to the Moon*. Travelers, hurled at the moon via a giant space cannon, captured aliens and returned to Earth. The novel spawned a number of other popular novels and movies that fueled the imagination of popular culture through the 1960s.[77]

But despite Verne's influence, we really have only one person to thank for galvanizing the United States' vast financial and scientific resources and committing them to our first lunar mission: President John F. Kennedy.

Kennedy wasn't a scientist. He was a pragmatic political leader. He saw the wisdom of lunar exploration and the space program as a national imperative. Why was it so important? The truth is that Americans were jolted into action by Russian advances in the field.

The month before President Kennedy addressed Congress and called for an acceleration of the space program, Russia's Yuri Gagarin became the first human to orbit Earth. Weeks before Kennedy's speech, American astronaut Alan Shepard became the first American in space.

Kennedy, concerned with the rapid progress the Russians were making in space, declared space exploration a national priority and an important front that could help curtail communist ambitions.[78]

Kennedy's famous speech, given during a joint session of Congress on May 25, 1961, challenged US scientists to land a man on the moon.[79] What Kennedy needed to propel the United States in front of the Soviets was a game changer—what the *Harvard Business Review* calls a transformational innovation. Transformational innovations are required when you are trying to solve problems never solved before, using inventions that don't exist—such as sending humans to another planet.[80] Transformational innovations are common requirements for most moonshots.

Kennedy's national call to action came at a perilous time. The Cold War was in full swing after a decade-long arms race with the Soviet Union and a series of political and military confrontations in Europe and Asia. Now space was seen as the next potential conflict zone.

There was another more immediate concern—the United States was falling behind in technology needed to deliver intercontinental ballistic missiles (ICBMs). The US and Soviet space programs were closely tied to the development of ICBMs, and there was concern that if the Soviets had an advantage in space, it might give them an advantage in ICBMs and nuclear superiority.[81]

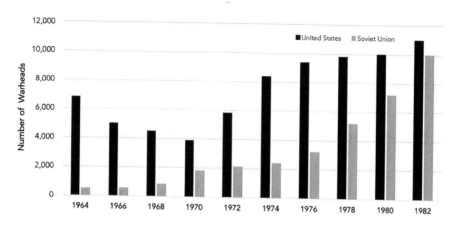

Nuclear Warheads: United States vs. Soviet Union[82, 83]

Rocket technology used for space missions would help perfect American ICBM technology. One scientist summarized early rocket technology by stating, "we were basically taking the nuclear warhead off a missile and putting a space capsule on it."[84] Every mission in space helped to improve and test US missile technology.

Some of the missions had a dual purpose. For example, astronaut Gordon Cooper spent much of his time during the Mercury 7 mission using instruments to detect and photograph Russian nuclear-launch sites.[85]

You can imagine the American mood during the early 1960s. American nuclear superiority and conventional military might were being challenged everywhere. After emerging victorious from World War II, Americans quickly found themselves fighting a new adversary. The Soviet Union caught up with US technical capabilities and produced its own atom bomb.

A sense of distress and extreme anxiety gripped the United States. In their book *America Divided*, authors Maurice Isserman and Michael Kazan describe that Americans "feared that a new and even more devastating world war—fought with nuclear weapons—could break out at any time. Affluence might suddenly give way to annihilation. The backdrop to the '60s was thus a society perched between great optimism and great fear."[86]

The Russian advantage in the early space race contributed to America's growing security anxiety. Developing the technology needed to achieve the lofty goals of putting a man on the moon before the end of the decade—the essence of the space race— became a national security priority.

Kennedy took ownership of problem that the United States was falling behind in developing rocket technology and created an enlightened, structured approach for solving the problem. He marshaled the available resources, centralized the strategy, and leaned on the experts to develop and refine their strategy as the initiative evolved.

It was clear that incremental improvements would not help America dominate in space; the United States needed an ambitious program that leapfrogged the Soviets. After consulting with Vice President Johnson and NASA Administrator James Webb, Kennedy believed that the lunar missions were the answer. "Only the construction of the Panama Canal in modern peacetime and the Manhattan Project in war were comparable in scope" to sending man to the moon.[87] Clearly, NASA needed a strategy to achieve its ambitious objective.

The Mercury, Gemini, and Apollo space missions were designed to execute Kennedy's goal. Mercury's six missions, flown between 1961 and 1963, focused on perfecting the process of sending human beings into space. These missions tested our ability to function in space and to retrieve a spacecraft and its occupants safely.[88]

Gemini's ten missions flew between 1964 and 1966 and propelled the US space program ahead of the Soviets for the first time.[89] The missions focused on longer-duration missions and tested orbiting and docking methods along with reentry techniques. Gemini missions also helped test how astronauts would hold up under longer missions in space.[90]

The seventeen Apollo missions between 1967 and 1972 sent humans to the moon on six separate occasions and solidified American dominance in the space race.[91] Before humans could walk on another planet for the first time, NASA needed to perfect its abilities to conduct research and operate on another world. The focus of the first ten missions was to test US capabilities for landing and operating on the lunar surface.[92]

Program:	Mercury	Gemini	Apollo
Years:	1959-1963	1964-1966	1967-1972
Missions:	6	10	6
Main Accomplishments:	Launched first American in space and earth orbit	Test long duration mission capability	Launched first human on the moon

Race to the Moon: Mercury, Gemini, and Apollo Missions

Each mission helped test and evolve technology and techniques needed to send astronauts to the moon, land them on it, and retrieve them from it, solving problems with solutions never before attempted.

Kennedy's assassination prevented him from seeing his goal come to life when, on July 20, 1969, Neil Armstrong climbed down off the Apollo 11 Lunar Module and onto the moon's surface. The lunar missions propelled the United States ahead in space and gave it an unparalleled advantage in space and beyond.

Many of the technologies developed to fly the Apollo missions would influence consumer products for decades. As NASA flight director Glynn Lunney witnessed, "Apollo really did drive our industry. We were asking people to do things that were probably 10 or

20 years faster than they otherwise would have done. And they knew it. They stepped up to it and succeeded. Today's cell phones, wireless equipment, iPads and so on are a result of the fact that the country did this hi-tech thing and created this large portfolio of available technologies."[93]

The results show what happens when we pursue a true objective with focus, dedication, and ingenuity, accomplishing a goal previously thought impossible. The solutions developed in the American effort to send astronauts to the moon created new technologies and enhanced American military superiority. The program achieved the aims Kennedy laid out in his call to action, relied on the enlightened leadership of Presidents Kennedy and Johnson and the experts at NASA (among others), and was fueled by a strategy that dynamically evolved with each launch.

Whether American military superiority was truly in jeopardy or the Soviets would have dominated the world if JFK had not challenged the nation to mobilize, we just don't know. But we do know one of America's most perilous challenges resulted in a moonshot focused on saving world democracy. Defeating fascism in the 1930s and 1940s was indeed an American imperative. Fascism threatened every single principle our democracy—and our European allies—held dear.

VI

Defeating Fascism

The Cold War was so prolific it affected the American psyche for more than a generation. While the threat of nuclear war was sometimes real and the global battle between communism and capitalism lasted decades, it is easy to forget the Cold War followed closely on the heels of an epic battle between fascism and our liberal democratic way of life. When the United States entered World War II, the Allied path to victory was less than certain.

Fascist regimes stand in stark contrast to liberal democracies that seek to curb the tyranny of the majority and preserve individual rights. Fascism flourishes when a single political party prioritizes national unity in a totalitarian state.[94] Life was perilous for most people in the 1930s. It was a decade "that was haunted by mass poverty and violent extremism," and its aftermath was the "darkest, bloodiest chapter in human history."[95]

Many called World War I the "war to end all wars" because it promised to create a new political global dynamic. Post–World War I Europe saw a rise in liberal democratic governments as self-determination increased across the continent. The economic crisis of the 1930s, the burdensome stipulations heaped upon the losers, and the rise of socialism all contributed to a series of crises that imperiled many of the fledgling democracies in Europe. Fascists seized on the chaos, unleashing "their militants in order to make democracy unworkable and discredit the constitutional state...then posed as the only non-socialist force that could restore order."[96]

Fascists despised key liberal democratic principles such as equal protection of human rights; political freedoms for all citizens; and free, fair, and competitive promotion of different ideas. In truth, fascism allowed "a new recipe for governing with popular support but without any sharing of power with the Left."[97] Socialists were gaining massive political support during the economic crisis of the 1930s. At the time, conservatives held the keys to power across Europe but were being challenged by the wave of populism that threatened stability and paralyzed Europe. In his book *The Anatomy of Fascism*, Robert Paxton writes that without deadlocked governments, "no fascist movement is likely to reach office."[98]

Germany after World War I felt national shame and was crippled by economic and political instability. Italy was in the middle of great social upheaval as socialists became the dominant political force in the country after World War I.[99] Italian nationalists were still smarting from Italy's poor performance on the battlefield against the Austrians during World War I, where nearly six hundred thousand Italians died fighting to a stalemate.[100]

Fascists rose to power by fueling the flames of nationalism and resentment, promising to punish those responsible for Italy's shame and bring stability from the chaos.[101] Conservatives in Italy and Germany invited Hitler and Mussolini individually into governing coalitions, in the hopes of controlling their respective movements while retaining the keys of power. These coalitions were temporary stepping-stones to power that helped both leaders ultimately achieve absolute authority. Conservative leaders were later betrayed as both Mussolini and Hitler consolidated power.

Meanwhile, in 1930s Japan, tension between traditionalists who supported the emperor and those who sought to impose limits to his power were the backdrop for the rise of fascism in Asia. Nationalists consolidated power after a coup by reformists failed,[102] and the fascist victors continued a campaign of nationalist militarism that sought to put all of Asia under the Japanese emperor's flag.

It is hard to imagine a more difficult challenge than going to war against Germany, Italy, and Japan at once. By the time the United States entered the war, more than half the world's population had submitted to the Axis powers, while another third fought desperately to remain free.[103]

America faced a difficult situation. The country's remaining allies, England and Russia, were faltering. Germany and Japan seemed unstoppable. Despite their battlefield successes both countries were aware that keeping the United States out of the war was necessary for their continued dominance. America had paid a heavy price for its involvement in World War I, and memories were still fresh of the sacrifices made during the war. The country was also exhausted from the Great Depression, and millions were still out of work when the English and French declared war on Germany.[104] America initially chose to stay out of the war, hoping the Europeans would be able to deal with German and Italian aggression on their own, without the need of another costly American intervention.

American hero Charles Lindbergh and his eight hundred thousand–strong America First movement opposed any US involvement in the war and made strong cases to remain neutral. The group "was harshly critical of the Roosevelt administration, which it accused of pressing the U.S. toward war. At its peak…[the movement] included socialists, conservatives, and some of the most prominent Americans from some of the most prominent families."[105]

At their height, the combined German, Japanese, and Italian armies wielded more than 18.5 million soldiers—making theirs the largest combined armed force ever assembled.[106, 107, 108] The sheer size of their combined armies and their battlefield successes would give any rational nation pause before entering the fray.

Before America joined the war, its citizens needed to be convinced inaction was more perilous than joining the allied cause.

President Roosevelt decided to make his case to the American people at the University of Virginia in Charlottesville. The campus, originally designed by Thomas Jefferson, had served as a proverbial American crossroads during pivotal times in our history—the Revolution, the Civil War, and now at the start of America's intervention in World War II. FDR made an impassioned plea, warning that America could not survive as a "lone island in a world dominated by the philosophy of force."[109] He made his case and then pledged to lend aid to those fighting the Axis powers and begin building up the American military defense, assuming one day we would enter the war.

The United States officially entered the war after Japan bombed the American Pacific fleet at Pearl Harbor in 1941. At the time, Britain and the Soviet Union were in rough shape. By 1942, Britain was close to defeat on every front, and the Soviet Union was in even worse shape. The Soviet tank battalions and air force were nearly destroyed, and two-thirds of its critical industrial capacity was behind enemy lines.[110]

As America entered the war, FDR, Churchill, and Stalin were the enlightened leaders whose call to action saved democracy across the world. It is worth pointing out that authoritarian Russia did not join the allied cause to promote democracy; rather, it joined out of a desire for self-preservation. At the same time, Churchill and FDR were not enamored with Stalin or the Soviet system but were smart enough to know they must unite to defeat fascism.

Defeating the Axis powers would not be easy and would require an immense effort. If we apply the analytical model we introduced earlier in the book, we can see a very clear, disciplined approach leading to the defeat of the Axis powers. We know several key facts that were influential in modeling an allied strategy that ultimately won the war:

- The potential collapse of the Soviet and English war-fighting capability was a possibility early in the war.

- America's economy was the largest on Earth, but the country's ability to challenge Germany on the battlefield was years away.
- Because of its sheer size, no one had ever successfully invaded and occupied Russia.
- Japan and Italy did not have modern industrial economies that compared with other Allied economies. Germany would be forced to rely on its own industrial capacity to fight the Allies.
- Most of Russia's industrial and agricultural capacity was west of the Urals and currently under German occupation.
- Germany needed oil to fuel its modern mechanized armies.

The strategy to defeat the Axis powers evolved over a series of more than two dozen meetings that spanned the length of the war.[111] Early conferences set the "European First" strategy and set up lend-lease and other aid for England and the Soviet Union. Conferences to organize the invasion of North Africa and the Italian campaigns came next, followed by planning for the D-Day invasion and the final strategy for defeating Germany and Japan. Gradually, the model for victory was built, and throughout the many campaigns that resulted in Allied victory, the strategy was fine-tuned and constantly refined.

While thousands of tactical decisions contributed to Allied victory, Joachim von Ribbentrop, Hitler's foreign minister, cited three major critical factors that hastened Germany's defeat. From his cell in Nuremberg, he wrote, "The unexpected 'power of resistance' of the Red Army; the vast supply of American armaments; and the success of Allied air power" were the keys to Germany's defeat.[112]

Hitler's fateful invasion of Russia was the beginning of the end of his thousand-year Reich. It is hard to imagine the scale of sheer destruction caused by the German invasion of the Soviet Union in 1941. Operation Barbarossa was one of the deadliest campaigns in human history. Nearly eight hundred thousand Russians were killed, and nearly six million were wounded or captured during the six-month campaign.

But losses on the German side were heavy too. The tenacity of the Russian defenses destroyed the Wehrmacht's battlefield superiority, reducing the number of offensive-capable units by nearly two-thirds.[113] The Germans weren't expecting fierce resistance or for Russian spirit to recover from such a massive operation. While the early campaign was clearly a crushing defeat for Stalin's Russia, the Red Army's fierce resistance forever eliminated Germany's ability to maintain the kind of battlefield superiority it had enjoyed in earlier campaigns in France and Poland. These losses made it difficult for the Germans to fight off the allies in North Africa, Italy, and eventually France.

While field power before Operation Barbarossa was a distinct advantage of the Axis powers, economic output was not. At the start of the war, the United States' gross domestic product alone was larger than the combined economic output of all three Axis nations.[114] America's vast industrial economy was the single largest advantage the country brought to the Allied cause. American economic output provided two critical advantages: First, lend-lease and other direct aid helped keep the Russians and English going during the early years of America's engagement. Second, in later years of the war, America's industrial capacity helped the Allies achieve and maintain massive aerial superiority and capability to supply the Allied armies.

America was clearly not ready for war as the conflict in Europe and Asia reached a flashing point. In 1939, the US Army ranked thirty-ninth in the world in size and possessed little of the mechanized mobility seen in the German Blitzkrieg.[115] It was, however, able to swing its mighty economy to a wartime footing and out produced its rivals. In the end, this capability won the war for the allies. The United States "provided almost two-thirds of all the Allied military equipment produced during the war: 297,000 aircraft, 193,000 artillery pieces, 86,000 tanks and two million army trucks."[116]

Economic output alone was not enough to win the Allied cause. Years of hard-fought battlefield victories were required to beat back the Germans, Italians, and Japanese. These victories, like those in Operation Barbarossa, helped deplete the Axis powers' ability to fight; meanwhile, the US economy kicked in and supplied the Allies with fresh planes, tanks, ships, and trucks to keep up the Allied momentum and pressure.

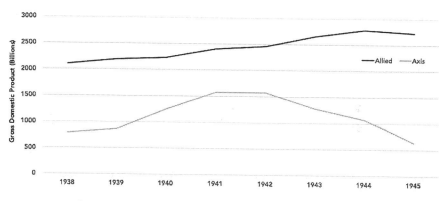

Gross Domestic Product, Axis vs. Allied Powers[117]

The Allies hoped devastating bombing campaigns targeting population centers would cause massive social upheaval and result in the German people rising up against the Nazi regime.[118] Of course, that never happened. Instead, the Allies inflicted massive carnage on the civilian population and had little effect on German industrial output until the final year of the war.[119] By the end of the war, millions were displaced by Allied bombing campaigns and ground war, and the European fascist threat was confined to history.

Despite the massive, overwhelming, and consequential victory achieved by the Allies in Europe, the war was far from over. Attention shifted to the Asian theater, and an all-out effort to defeat the Japanese began.

The road to defeating Japan began early in the war with a US victory at Guadalcanal. Americans began pushing from the south-west toward the Philippines and west from Hawaii across the Central Pacific. The British and Chinese began their assault from India and Burma.[120] Over the next three years of brutal warfare, Japan's empire was whittled away in a series of hard-fought battles that followed a prescribed path, gradually moving closer to the Japanese mainland. Eventually, Allied forces were within striking distance of the Japanese mainland, and a full-scale invasion was planned. With the Japanese threatened by invasion on two fronts from Russian and American forces, the options for negotiating better conditions for surrender were dwindling every day. After the bombings of Hiroshima and Nagasaki, the Japanese surrendered unconditionally in 1945.[121]

The war killed more than eighty million people. Both combatants and civilians were caught in the crossfire or died from famine or disease.[122] The true origin of all this evil and darkness started with a worldwide economic calamity that fanned the flames of nationalism. The feeling of fear was met with the fascists' aggressive agenda to make their countries better—creating an opening for authoritarians to take power. This shift led to the greatest existential crisis ever faced by the world's democracies.

The strategy developed to defeat fascism ultimately resulted in allied victory. It achieved the aims laid out in FDR's and Churchill's calls to action to save democracy. The world relied on the enlightened leadership of President Roosevelt, Prime Minister Churchill, and Premier Stalin (and so many others) and was fueled by a strategy that evolved with each battle taking advantage of the allies' economic superiority.

Not all moonshots require an existential crisis to promote action. Some are driven by other less-existential factors. Case in point: finding a way to eradicate polio became a priority stoked by fears of parents everywhere who were worried about their children.

VII

Eradicating Polio

Warm Springs, Georgia, was a relatively small, sleepy resort town in the early 1920s when Franklin Delano Roosevelt made his first visit there. He had been encouraged to visit and bathe in the springs that promised to help soothe his muscles, which were stiffened by paralysis. It was rare for adults to contract polio and rarer still for them to become paralyzed. Despite the odds, FDR was stricken with the disease and became paralyzed from the waist down. After his first swim in one of the soothing pools at Warm Springs, Roosevelt felt immediate relief and was able to move his right leg for the first time in three years.[123] He was so encouraged by the results that he bought resort property in the area and created the Warm Springs Foundation, which eventually evolved into the March of Dimes.

The March of Dimes' primary focus was to find a cure for polio and improve the standards of care for those stricken with the disease in the first half of the twentieth century. While today polio has been nearly eradicated, it is hard to imagine how fearful the world was of the disease at that time. While many more died from cancer and car accidents during the early twentieth century, people feared polio even more. In the years following World War II, polio fears in the United States were trumped only by the threat of nuclear attack.[124]

Evidence to support the existence of polio goes back thousands of years, but it doesn't show the types of mass epidemics common in the early twentieth century. The first epidemic in the United States was in Vermont in 1894, and within twenty years, New York City experienced an outbreak that infected twenty-seven thousand people and killed six thousand.[125] Late summer became polio season, and public-health advisories were issued to help limit the disease's spread. By 1952, nearly sixty thousand US children were diagnosed with polio; many were paralyzed, and three thousand died.[126]

The virus is transmitted from human-to-human contact or through contact with contaminated feces. The virus multiplies in the intestines and then spreads to the nervous system, sometimes resulting in paralysis.[127] Some believe these epidemics were hastened, not prevented, by the widespread improvements in sanitation that became common in the United States in the late nineteenth century.

Before that time, "virtually all children were infected with [polio] while still protected by maternal antibodies. In the 1900s, following the industrial revolution of the late 18th and early 19th centuries, improved sanitation practices led to an increase in the age at which children first encountered the virus, such that at exposure children were no longer protected by maternal antibodies. Consequently, epidemics of poliomyelitis surfaced."[128]

While scientists had been making vaccines for potentially thousands of years, they were not administered en masse until the late nineteenth century, when "antitoxins and vaccines against diphtheria, tetanus, anthrax, cholera, plague, typhoid, tuberculosis and others" were developed.[129]

These advancements were spawned by a new focus in the scientific community aimed at understanding and studying bacteria and viruses. The smallpox vaccine was developed by Edward Jenner, an English physician, who in 1796 perfected the technique for stimulating the body's natural defenses to prevent the disease. Louis Pasteur developed the rabies vaccine a century later.[130]

These early advancements were made during an era of nearly no government oversight or industry standards. It wasn't until 1902, when Congress created the Hygienic Laboratory of the US Public Health Service—now called the National Institutes of Health—that there was anybody responsible for setting standards for the safe manufacture of drugs.[131] The new regulations became necessary after two tetanus outbreaks from contaminated vaccines broke out in New Jersey and Missouri a year earlier.[132]

It is hard to imagine what the world today would be like if it weren't for Jonas Salk, who invented the world's first polio vaccine. Salk was the son of Russian-Jewish immigrants, and his father was a laborer in the New York garment district.[133, 134] Salk graduated from the New York University School of Medicine in 1939 and began working on vaccines in 1942. In 1947, he began work full-time on a polio vaccine at the University of Pittsburgh's School of Medicine, with funding from the March of Dimes Foundation.[135]

Prior to Salk, scientists believed that vaccines must use active versions of a virus in order to be successful. Live-virus vaccines with weakened cultures were problematic because they sometimes became strong enough to cause the actual disease.[136] Two New York University researchers' early attempts at creating a vaccine using live cultures provided no immunity and resulted in nine deaths out of ten thousand children inoculated.[137]

Salk's approach was contrary to popular scientific principles at the time. His research focused on growing samples of the virus and then "deactivating them by adding formaldehyde so that they could no longer reproduce."[138] By injecting the benign strains into the bloodstream, Salk hoped to summon the body's natural defenses, creating antibodies that would lead to immunity.

At the time, many scientists believed Salk's approach was a dead end. Many, including virologist Albert Sabin, believed the only way to prompt the body's natural defenses was with a "live-virus" vaccine. Sabin called Salk a "kitchen chemist," criticizing his approach and research.

Producing a live-virus vaccine was time-consuming, and many leading the charge for a polio vaccine were becoming extremely anxious. Polio cases were surging, and by the early 1950s, more than fifty thousand cases were reported in the United States each year, nearly half of which resulted in paralysis.[139]

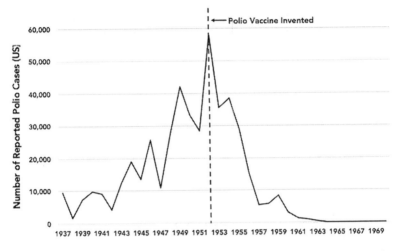

Reported US Polio Cases 1938–1970[140]

The rise in polio cases prompted President Truman to declare a nationwide emergency and call for what amounted to a nationwide polio moonshot when he said, "The fight against infantile paralysis cannot be a local war…It must be nationwide. It must be total war in every city, town and village throughout the land. For only with a united front can we ever hope to win any war."[141]

It is worth noting that none of this research would have been conducted without a massive parallel effort to help fund it. Two men, Franklin Roosevelt and his college friend Basil O'Connor, teamed up in 1924, ultimately raising more than seven billion dimes—more than a billion in today's dollars.[142] This money fueled research, helped improve therapies, and ultimately resulted in a vaccine that saved many from paralysis and death. Roosevelt and O'Conner were not scientists—they were outsiders on a mission. Their enlightened leadership created a groundswell that raised research money and awareness through the March of Dimes Foundation. Their efforts, along with those of Salk and Sabin, ultimately helped eradicate polio in the United States and around the world.

Ultimately, both live- and dead-virus methods resulted in vaccines. Salk's method was faster. He began trials in 1952 that were so promising that by 1954, he was authorized to conduct a nationwide trial. Nearly 1.3 million children were inoculated that year, and the results were wildly successful. Nearly 80 to 90 percent of those who were given an inoculation did not develop the disease.[137] The vaccine was licensed for general use the same day his results were announced. Today, dozens are diagnosed with polio each year in the United States, versus tens of thousands before Salk's vaccine became readily available in 1955.

It is worth noting that today's oral polio vaccine contains a live form of the virus perfected by Albert Sabin. Sabin didn't perfect his vaccine until 1960.[143] By then, Salk's vaccine had prevented an estimated two hundred thousand polio infections and saved thousands from paralysis and possible death.[144]

Part 3: Where Do We Focus?

VIII

Cybersecurity Moonshot Objectives

We spent the first three chapters of this book reviewing the grim state of cybersecurity and the overall complexity of the problem. We know cybercrime is growing exponentially, has touched the majority of Americans, and shows no signs of abating. But how do we begin to solve this highly complex problem? If there is anything to learn from our review of efforts to reach the moon, defeat the Nazis, and cure polio, half measures will not do. Our moonshot must be comprehensive, involve key players, and transform the cybersecurity landscape.

Perhaps it is worth first investigating common breach causes. The 2017 Verizon Data Breach Report, the most comprehensive analysis of data breaches available, found a small number of key factors common across the breaches in their study. They found more than half of breaches over the last seven years involved some use of one or more of the following techniques: hacking, malware propagation, or use of stolen and/or weak passwords.[145]

Where do cybersecurity experts feel most vulnerable? Let's look at areas where they are making investments. According to a recent SANS Institute survey of technology executives, application/data security, access management, advanced malware protection, and endpoint protection are the most important initiatives.[146]At first glance, it appears that company cybersecurity spending aligns with the areas the Verizon study shows are the weakest—a very optimistic sign.

Studying common breach causes and cybersecurity priorities helps us filter and focus our model on the conditions, causes, and solutions that will contribute most to our moonshot. Preventing application-security vulnerabilities that contribute to so many breaches and addressing the human factors contributing to cybersecurity issues will be key to our moonshot.

Changing behaviors of key actors will also be an important dynamic. While threat actors are central to the cybersecurity landscape, they will not positively contribute to our overall moonshot. We don't have to look any further than the technology supply chain to help us identify the key players we will need to draft into this effort. Software vendors, buyers, and end users are all stakeholders in the cybersecurity landscape, but they each have different roles to play in our moonshot. We also propose introducing a new player who has been absent from this fight from the start: the government.

How do software vendors, buyers, end users, and the government come together in a comprehensive cybersecurity moonshot? It is worth looking to our other moonshot examples for inspiration.

The most important element of any moonshot initiative is centralized, purposeful action. Whether it is improving ballistic missile technology by investing in the space program, saving democracy by defeating fascism, or eradicate polio, each successful objective was defined by a common set of priorities coordinated from beginning to end by a central authority. NASA coordinated the lunar program, the Allied command collaborated intensely against the Axis powers, and the March of Dimes funded the promising researchers who led to the polio vaccine. We will need a central champion to coordinate our cybersecurity moonshot too.

Once our organizational champion is identified, it must focus on solutions that address the core problems of application security and the human factors contributing to cybersecurity issues. The solution model we propose in later chapters must align key stakeholders in a coordinated set of parallel efforts to realize the full potential of our moonshot objectives.

Technology is global. A look at the top technology companies finds a mix of US, Chinese, South Korean, and Japanese companies dominating the top fifteen spots in 2016.[147] But a closer look reveals that three US companies—Apple, Google, and Microsoft—are the most dominant technology players on Earth. Their software platforms—iOS, Android, and Windows—run on billions of Internet-connected devices, including mobile phones, computers, and tablets. They are so influential that they can help move the market. Our cybersecurity moonshot must have their buy-in to be successful. Because the most dominant players in the tech ecosystem call the United States home, it is natural to expect the US government might play a critical role in helping to coordinate our cybersecurity moonshot.

The US federal government has been hesitant to step in and lead the effort to improve cybersecurity. So far, the work has been lackluster and far from cohesive. Individual agencies launched industry-focused regulations such as HIPAA (Health and Human Services), FedRamp (Department of Homeland Security, Department of Justice, and General Services Administration), FERC (Department of Energy), and the Cybersecurity Framework (National Institutes of Standards and Technology). These individual efforts created a hodgepodge of regulatory requirements but have not helped address fundamental cybersecurity challenges. Still, there is a role for the federal government in leading this moonshot, but it will take dynamic leadership to drive meaningful progress.

Technology suppliers must be incentivized by the market and by government programs that disrupt the current paradigm, where speed to market is the essential driving element of product strategy. As we learned in chapter 1, the speed-to-market paradigm has been in effect for decades, and changing it will be no small feat. Apple and Google, among the wealthiest tech companies, spend millions on lobbying lawmakers.[148] Historically, most companies try to lobby against restrictive or punitive regulations, so our moonshot will have to use incentives rather than penalties to help promote healthy cybersecurity practices. If we create the right market conditions that favor cybersecurity innovation and do not threaten the dominance of key players, we'll be more likely to win their support.

We must also find a way to align technology suppliers and buyers in the common effort of solving key cybersecurity challenges. Right now, a small number of technology suppliers have most of the power in the world—especially in the small world of software operating systems. For Microsoft, Google, and Apple, there is nearly no threat of substitution, there are very few rivals to compete with, and there is a high cost of change from one software operating system to another.

If we follow Porter's Five Forces, which model behaviors in competitive landscape, the only lever available to alter the competitive behavior in a major software universe is to leverage the collective power of buyers to influence the security landscape.

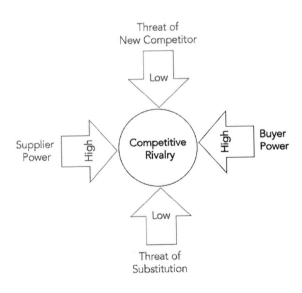

Porter's Five Forces

To influence buyer behavior, corporate leaders and board members need to take an increasing role in demanding better cybersecurity from their organizations. Corporate leaders must set high standards, invest wisely in cybersecurity, and expect more secure solutions from vendors—all critical elements needed to support our moonshot.

All the other actions we have discussed so far are moot if we don't also come up with solutions to address the human factors that contribute to poor cybersecurity. Humans are fallible, and no level of awareness training will completely protect them from social-engineering tactics that hackers rely on. Technology users number in the billions globally—estimates indicate there were 2.6 billion Internet-connected smartphones and two billion computers in use globally in 2015—and educating all or some of them is beyond comprehension.[149, 150] We have figured out how to make tech enabled devices intuitive and usable for billions of people, with little to no training. If we want to solve the human element of cybersecurity, we have to make security as intuitive as the very technology it sits on.

IX

Software

We established earlier that the commercial software market has traditionally favored speed to market over security. While commercial software vendors have made strides to improve security, it has not been enough to make software safe from hackers. As we explored in chapter 2, operating systems and other commercial software are becoming more complex, and the truth is the rate of new vulnerabilities are not growing at the same rate. That may mean we are making some progress improving security in commercial software, but we know it is not enough.

While Microsoft committed to invest more than $1 billion per year in cybersecurity research and development, much of that spending is used to make its flagship Windows security software better.[151] Microsoft's Trustworthy Computing Security Development Lifecycle was designed to ensure security was included in its software-development and release process. While the process has gone a long way in reducing security software bugs, Microsoft is still forced to schedule and release patches monthly to fix security and other issues.[152]

It is not fair to pick on Microsoft. No technology company or solution is immune to this problem. An analysis of the top ten security flaws by vendor shows that the world's most popular commercial software is full of thousands of holes. The vendors with the highest concentration of vulnerabilities include different flavors of the Linux operating system, including software provided by Linux, Apple, Ubuntu, and Google. Many in the technology world falsely believe Linux products to be more secure and often favor them over Microsoft products.

Vendor	Nbr of Products	Nbr of Vulnerabilities	Nbr of Vulnerabilities / #Products
Linux	15	1,952	130
Mozilla	21	1,718	82
Google	58	2,876	50
Canonical	23	871	38
Apple	115	3,916	34
Adobe	120	2,392	20
Novell	118	1,532	13
Debian	89	1,151	13
Microsoft	456	5,279	12
Oracle	470	4,607	10
SUN	204	1,630	8
Redhat	238	1,593	7
IBM	895	3,557	4
Cisco	1,784	3,137	2
HP	2,037	1,412	1

Cumulative Vulnerabilities by Vendor, 1999–2017[153]

Where commercial products fail to meet the market's demands for better application security, others follow. A vibrant community focusing on application security has begun to flourish. Groups like the Open Web Application Security Project (OWASP) have focused on providing access to training materials and other resources designed to help increase awareness of application security issues. The hope is awareness will help yield improved application security. OWASP publishes a top-ten list of dedicated-to-web application security issues every few years. An analysis of application security issues from its 2010, 2013, and 2017 lists finds little change in the top security issues for web applications. More than half of the vulnerabilities on the top ten list in 2010 remained on the list seven years later.

2010	2013	2017
A1 Injection	A1 Injection	A1 Injection
A2 Cross-Site Scripting (XSS)	A2 Broken Authentication and Session Management	A2 Broken Authentication
A3 Broken Authentication and Session Management	A3 Cross-Site Scripting (XSS)	A3 Sensitive Data Exposure
A4 Insecure Direct Object References	A4 Insecure Direct Object References	**A4 XML External Entities (XXE)**
A5 Cross-Site Request Forgery (CSRF)	A5 Security Misconfiguration	**A5 Broken Access Control**
A6 Security Misconfiguration	*A6 Sensitive Data Exposure*	A6 Security Misconfiguration
A7 Insecure Cryptographic Storage	**A7 Missing Function Level Access Control**	A7 Cross-Site Scripting (XSS)
A8 Failure to Restrict URL Access	A8 Cross-Site Request Forgery (CSRF)	**A8 Insecure Deserialization**
A9 Insufficient Transport Layer Protection	**A9 Using Components with Known Vulnerabilities**	A9 Using Components with Known Vulnerabilities
A10 Unvalidated Redirects and Forwards	A10 Unvalidated Redirects and Forwards	**A10 Insufficient Logging & Monitoring**

Key: **Bold** = New; *Italicized* = Merged

OWASP Top Ten Web Application Vulnerabilities, 2010–2017[154]

If large programmatic efforts to improve security and open-source educational initiatives are not enough to move the software-security needle, what other options do we have? Certainly, no single approach will solve such a complex problem, but perhaps we can get some inspiration from two men named Merrill and Mudge.

William Henry Merrill was best known for founding the Underwriters Electrical Bureau in 1894, which later became known as Underwriters Laboratories (UL). Most people aren't aware of the role UL played in making the world safer by developing technical standards and testing to help improve the safety of nearly everything we plug into an electrical outlet.

Many may be familiar, however, with the UL Listed logo, indicating that a product has met the Underwriters Laboratories gold standard for safety. UL claims its mark has adorned more than twenty-two billion products, certifying they have met one or more of the sixteen hundred safety standards it has developed over its lifetime.[155] While these are impressive numbers, the most important fact is that UL safety standards have saved thousands of lives. UL is central to product safety in the United States because it "works with Federal agencies to set minimum voluntary safety standards for industries where mandatory regulations are absent...because of liability concerns...few manufacturers of electrical goods will market them without UL's seal."[156]

While UL's history isn't perfect, it fills an important gap in developing standards for products in areas where the government lacks comfort or experience in regulating.

While Merrill's legacy helped make billions of products safer, Mudge hoped to help make code more secure. As part of the infamous hacking collective L0ft, he helped expose the true cybersecurity dangers to the Senate back in 1998. While L0ft's dire warning went unheeded, its mission to introduce better cybersecurity practices and standards lived on.

Mudge, whose real name is Peiter Zaiko, has had a storied career working for the Defense Advanced Research Project Agency (DARPA) and Google's ATAP skunk works. He left Google in 2016 at the request of the White House to help establish the Cyber Independent Testing Laboratory with seed funding from DARPA.[157] The idea behind Cyber-ITL was to create standards and testing schemes using the Underwriters Laboratories model for inspiration. Its goals were admirable and lofty. In a 2015 interview with the Council on Foreign Relations,[158] Mudge listed his top four goals for Cyber-ITL as the following:

- Consumers having the ability to comparatively distinguish safe products from unsafe and secure from insecure;
- Pressure on developers to harden their products and engage in defensive development practices;
- The ability to quantify risk; and

- Take away low-hanging fruit, such as the more insecure product-development practices, and thus begin to devalue parts of the exploit market.

While Cyber-ITL has yet to make its mark on cybersecurity as a whole, it does present an interesting opportunity to introduce transparency and create market pressures to improve commercial software and hardware security.

The ability to create software free of security bugs will be a difficult endeavor, and we shouldn't invest all our energies in one moonshot initiative. There are other solutions we could explore to help us improve software security. DARPA funded the Cyber Grand Challenge, which brought security innovators and hackers together in a competition that pitted self-healing software against rogue attackers. The goal was to perform a real-life evaluation, testing the concept of autonomous cyber defense in a real-world attack scenario.[159] Could systems be trained to detect attacks and fix vulnerabilities on the fly, limiting hackers' ability to breach networks and cause havoc?

The intense, three-year exercise was capped off in the final Cyber Grand Challenge capture-the-flag event held in Las Vegas during the 2016 DEF CON cybersecurity conference. The results were clear. Mike Walker, who managed the DARPA program, felt "enormously gratified that we achieved CGC's primary goal, which was to provide clear proof of principle that machine-speed, scalable cyber defense is indeed possible."[160]

If the concept of self-healing code in the marketplace will come in only a matter of time, can we begin to contemplate a world free from security bugs altogether?

Deep learning platforms (DLPs) likely will be able to develop and recognize patterns in risky software code by learning from known good and known bad sample sets. DLPs consisting of "artificial neural networks with multiple abstraction layers…used in pattern recognition" are showing some promise but are still in the early stages of development.[161]

It is likely that DLP platforms can help identify and fix software vulnerabilities before they hit the marketplace, making it harder for hackers to use software as a way to breach networks and computers. The key appeal for the adaptation of these types of tools is the ability to improve speed to market and to reduce the total cost of maintaining software throughout its life cycle by reducing the number of patches that need to be issued.

Enhanced speed to market and a reduction in the total cost of ownership for vendors and consumers alike are game changers. Software companies that are early adopters will be poised to gain market advantage over their rivals. If these dynamics evolve, companies that produce nearly bug-free code in their software-development life cycles will become more common. As consumers recognize that software with fewer bugs is cheaper to operate in the long run, they will begin to give preference to vendors who incorporate these practices. Marrying these enhanced software-development techniques and introducing self-healing capabilities introduced in the DARPA experiment along with independent testing becomes a compelling way for vendors to dramatically reduce or eliminate security software flaws.

We must be cautious in assuming that self healing and DLP technologies are a panacea for fixing security vulnerabilities in the software supply chain. We have seen so many promising technologies come and go, often with the promise to fix complex problems. We also must realize that at the current rate of development and execution, self-healing code and bug-free code are decades away from making a difference without a concentrated moonshot-like effort.

We must also be realistic about acknowledging that two other major pillars must be addressed to comprehensively address cybersecurity challenges. If we fix code without making security intuitive or creating the right incentives for vendors to change, our moonshot will not be successful.

X

People

It's hard to have a comprehensive dialogue about how to fix cyber-security without understanding the role humans play in knowingly or unknowingly contributing to poor cybersecurity practices. Much has been written on the threat from malicious or unsuspecting insiders deep inside companies or on the general lack of cyber-security awareness among most technology users. While solving those problems is important, we're going to investigate solutions focused on securing digital identities and helping people avoid common social-engineering tactics used by criminals to lure them into cyber traps.

Social engineering is not new. It is an art finely crafted by con art-ists throughout the ages. In the digital world, social engineering has gained scale, allowing hackers and con artists alike to reach larger audiences. Social engineering typically involves using techniques to trick someone into revealing private information or engaging in an activity they would not normally participate in. Hackers take advan-tage of the fact that people are inherently trustful, often using offi-cial-looking e-mails to trick unsuspecting individuals into revealing sensitive information such as passwords or social security numbers.

Many high-profile data breaches started with fake e-mails, using a technique known as phishing. Hackers use e-mail because it allows them to scale attacks to thousands or even millions of potential victims in a single campaign. Phishing e-mails often use social-engineering techniques to trick users into clicking on malicious links or attachments sent via e-mail that often infect computers or direct users to malicious sites that prompt them to enter their usernames and passwords. Phishing is so pervasive that leading researchers believe it is costing American companies and consumers $500 million a year, and the cost continues to rise dramatically.[162]

Embedding smarter, adaptive machine learning or artificial-intelligence technologies inside malware and spam detection might help. Researchers believe that "AI and machine learning are being used to power more things in our lives than we're even aware of... the reason we need to rely on an AI instead of people is because of the massive amounts of data that needs to be processed and the speed at which machines can analyze data and connect the dots. Combating malware is no different."[163]

While reducing malware and phishing will help reduce risk of breaches and digital identity theft, it will not solve the digital-security challenge alone. A more comprehensive approach is required.

Today, the average person has dozens of online accounts made up of e-mail, social media, financial services, ecommerce, data/file sharing, and other types of accounts.[164, 165, 166] These accounts, along with other types of services such as credit files, make up an individual's digital identity. Most of these online accounts are secured using a username and password. The challenge is that passwords are no longer an effective mechanism to secure accounts. Password reuse is common across sites as users struggle to remember and maintain unique passwords. In a recent research study, more than half of respondents admitted that they reused passwords regularly and/or used less-complicated passwords to make it easier to remember.[167]

The main problem is that too much faith has been placed on passwords and social security numbers; neither was designed to be used across the digital universe we have today. Digital identity sprawl, similar to the problem that many companies face with their growing technology footprint, affects everyone who relies on technology to shop, bank, communicate, and learn. A Pew Research study found nearly 64 percent of Americans were the victims of some sort of data theft at one point in their lives.[168]

While social security numbers help facilitate "seamless digital access to financial services and credit...[allowing] millions of consumers [to] open a bank account or get approved for a credit card," they were never designed to "become the cornerstone of Americans' financial lives."[169] Breaches at Equifax and other financial services companies highlight the dangers of using central identifiers if they are not properly protected. The Equifax breach alone exposed social security numbers and personal financial information on more than 145 million individuals and highlighted how important social security numbers are to the financial system.[170]

Recent breaches exposing passwords have been helpful to hackers who often try stolen usernames and passwords on other sites. When professional networking site LinkedIn was breached in 2012, hackers cross-referenced passwords and employment history that led, in at least one instance, to further breaches. Hackers were able to log in to Dropbox's corporate network after hackers tried a Dropbox employee's LinkedIn password on the company's login site. Customers rely on Dropbox's secure platform to share files online, and hackers logged in to the Dropbox network and hacked their way into the company's password repository. This gave them access to millions of accounts and private files belonging to users of Dropbox's secure file-storage service.[171]

Security professionals recommend using multi-factor authentication (MFA) to protect online accounts by adding a layer of security to the login process. While MFA—for example, the use of a username, password, and one-time code sent to the user via text message or mobile application—is stronger than just a username and password, it is far from a perfect solution.

Signaling System No. 7 (SS7), the platform used to route calls and text messages between mobile phone companies, has major security flaws. Sophisticated hackers have found ways to penetrate SS7 and intercept phone calls and text messages, including the one-time codes sent via text in multi-factor authentication.[172] Further, mobile phones are so laden with malware that application-based MFA is no longer secure.[173]

It is clear that passwords are no longer a useful way to protect an individual's online accounts. Two promising trends are beginning to address online account security in a comprehensive and user-friendly way. First, single sign-on technologies are gaining traction across the web, leaving the complex management of user identity and access management to a few highly competent organizations. The second is that many companies are developing complex hardware and behavioral-based mechanisms in lieu of passwords to authenticate users. No matter where we end up, centralized authentication and identity-management platforms must be interoperable (usable by many applications from many different companies), secure, flexible, and mobile friendly.[174]

Several leading technology companies have been building out massive platforms that allow users to take advantage of using one login site (or provider) to help them log in to multiple other platforms. Google, Facebook, Microsoft, and Twitter standardized their platforms using an open standard called OAuth. As authentication platforms go, OAuth and a standard called OpenID Connect create a compelling, user-friendly authentication platform that simplifies identity and access management. While consolidating authentication platforms might reduce the number of passwords users might have to remember, it certainly does not solve the problem on its own.

Google's Abacus experiment and its Trust API platform are other steps in the right direction. They use behavioral analytics and sensors from Google smartphones to create behavioral patterns that are unique to an individual user.[175] Over time, Google's smartphone creates a trust score that is integrated with the company's authentication platform. Applications and websites both inside Google and outside the company can use its single sign-on platform to authenticate users. High-risk sites such as banking and e-mail might require a high degree of trust and require that more factors—including a recognized device, a biometric scan, and so on—beyond username and password be validated before a user is allowed to authenticate. Other sites, such as mobile gaming apps, may require a low level of trust to authenticate users.[176]

Centralized identity providers, coupled with mobile-phone technology, have enabled complex identity validation to offer a way to simplify the complexity of managing passwords. Putting too much faith in mobile devices, without addressing the fundamental security flaws in the software that runs them is risky. It is also risky to rely on a small number of identity providers to secure online identities because putting too much faith in a few companies could lead to a breach impacting a large number of people. Today, identity-providers companies give few security or privacy guarantees when we use their products. As we become more reliant on these centralized providers to help us protect our digital identities, we have to ask ourselves if it is time for the government to step in and require better security and privacy guarantees.

XI

Government

Suggesting government become more active in regulating tech companies as part of our moonshot initiative will not be very popular. A Pew Research Center survey found four in five Americans don't trust the federal government to perform effectively.[177] Gallup has been tracking the approval ratings of both Congress and the executive branch for decades, and both remain historically low.[178, 179]

While distrustful of the federal bureaucracy, Congress, and the president, Americans are united in their belief that the federal government's primary mission is to protect the general public from harm or to help in an emergency, such as terrorism or natural disasters.[180] Expecting the federal government to step in and protect the American public and lead our proposed cybersecurity moonshot is one thing; actually seeing the feds step up and lead is another.

The federal government is experiencing a crisis of confidence in helping to lead the way on cyber issues. The government contains too few experts, and those who exist are too far from the centers of power to make a meaningful difference in shaping policy. The problem is there is no alternative to federal-government leadership of our moonshot objective. No industry collective, no international organization, and no civic group has the reach and authority to lead our moonshot. If we have learned anything from our other moonshot lessons, the federal government will have to align executive and legislative priorities to be effective.

Policy czars are nothing new and have been standard practice going back to the FDR administration.[181] Centralizing policy development under a single individual might be our best shot at helping promote a standard national cybersecurity moonshot program.

For any policy czar to be effective, he or she will need bipartisan support, full authority to set federal cybersecurity policy and spending priorities, and an ability to maintain a working relationship in the business community. Effective policy czars offer the opportunity to provide for more "comprehensive planning and decision-making" across federal agencies.[182]

While President Obama appointed a number of policy czars, he received criticism from members of Congress for not routing the majority of his appointments through Senate confirmation hearings.[183] Obtaining formal congressional support for a cybersecurity moonshot czar will be highly important, since much of the work needed to align the effort will be policy driven and require a series of legislative initiatives. Another common criticism is that policy czars don't have "budget control or other real authority, and are often caught up in turf battles among Cabinet secretaries and fellow West Wingers,"[184] making the positions less effective. For the cybersecurity czar to be effective, he or she must be given "cabinet-like" authority to drive policy and behavior changes toward constructive outcomes that support our moonshot.

The cybersecurity czar will have to effectively address a number of key issues in our proposed moonshot. We discussed earlier in this book the importance of identifying and shifting norms as part of our effort to address complex problems. Ultimately, the czar will be focused on changing norms in the software world (speed-to-market wins), government (focused on offensive cyber priorities), corporations (cybersecurity is a tactical issue), and among the general public (security is burdensome). Creating government policies that promote market-driven incentives to improve cybersecurity, change toxic behaviors, and correct government misdeeds will need to be high priorities.

Ultimately, the cyber conundrum will get solved when long-standing norms that are driving unproductive behavior change. Norms "are rules of conduct that govern interactions" among key groups.[185] These norms drive powerful forces that influence behavior in everyday life, influencing outcomes that affect our conundrum. If we are going to be effective at addressing the conundrum, we have to design policies that change group and/or individual behaviors. These changes require new policy tools that do not exist today.

As H. Peyton Young of the Brookings Institution wrote when changing norms, "two are of particular importance are: i) the social network, that is, the web of connections that describe who interacts with whom; and ii) the mechanism by which norms of behavior are enforced by the group."[186]

The cybersecurity czar's first task is to align the public and private sectors in a series of initiatives that realigns norms into more constructive behaviors. The czar would use government and market forces to change behaviors through economic instruments designed to effect change and influence behavior.[187] We have seen many examples of how creating economic incentives can drive behavior in society and in the business world; mortgage deductions, 401(k)s, accounting rules, and tax rates have all been used to create incentives or penalties for certain behaviors. We'll focus here on ways to create incentives that drive positive market change. We find that "economic incentives are often contrasted to 'command and control' policy approaches that determine pollution reduction targets and define allowable control technologies via laws or regulations. In reality, however, command and control policy and economic incentives frequently operate in tandem."[188]

The first instrument to consider is the creation of economic incentives to encourage technology companies to build security into the products and services they sell. While tax incentives seem like an easy answer, giving tax breaks to wealthy companies to create incentives for something people believe they should be already doing will be a hard sell to the American public and to Congress. Perhaps liability waivers and potentially full liability protection might be a way to create the appropriate incentives. Companies spend billions of dollars a year on insurance, protecting themselves from cybersecurity liability.[189] Creating product or full-company protection from cybersecurity-related lawsuits might be a viable trade-off if companies demonstrate they can maintain a measure of auditable security proficiency tied to an industry best-practice standard.

Developing an evolving set of cybersecurity standards and certification processes for private industry has not been a traditional area of expertise for the federal government. There are a number of international standards bodies (e.g., AICPA, PCI, and CSA) that have developed a series of best practices and audit schemes designed to measure cybersecurity competency. They can be used to set minimum standards to qualify for incentives, and they could also develop new standards as technologies evolve.

Demonstrating cybersecurity competency and obtaining certifications can be used as a market differentiator and also serve as a minimum standard for corporate buyers and consumers alike. Much the same way Underwriters Laboratories established a standard used by companies globally today, standards organizations can help drive improved cybersecurity through testing against a set of industry-accepted best practices.

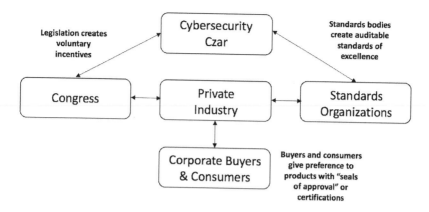

Cybersecurity Market-Incentives Model

Imagine the impact of a market based incentives model on how companies buy software and vendors prioritize the use of cyber-security best practices. Corporate buyers and consumers giving preference to software vendors and/or service providers that have secure products certified to stand up to hackers would be a potentially compelling proposition.

Will these incentives work to drive the types of behavioral changes and norms we need? Some might say incentives alone without penalties will always introduce incomplete results. Others believe incentives don't work at all or drive the wrong behavior. As one author studying incentives put it, while "the reward itself may be highly desired…[the] experience of being controlled is likely to assume a punitive quality over time."[190] It is possible that enhancing security will stifle the speed to market, but successful companies that quickly adapt to the new paradigm will have a market advantage.

Another area of opportunity lies with the realignment of the government's cybersecurity priorities. We learned in an earlier chapter that the federal government spends 90 percent of its cybersecurity funding on offensive operations and defending the government sector and 10 percent on law enforcement and protecting the private sector. In the interconnected world of cyberspace, companies are left to defend themselves against a whole host of determined enemies, including nation-states. We know of no other area where the private sector is expected to protect itself from a foreign foe.

We also learned from an earlier chapter that private industry is at extreme risk in the future from sustained cyberattack. Cyberwarfare tactics are being perfected in anticipation for a day when a conventional or hybrid war with the United States and/or other Western powers becomes a reality. No country is capable of sustaining prolonged economic, social, and/or political disruption from war. Cyber warfare introduces a new front where economic, social, and political disruption will be a key strategic element for our future adversaries. Knowing that reality, doesn't it make sense to shift the way we plan to defend ourselves?

First, we should consider how to protect private-company technology infrastructure and realign government priorities to focus on defense rather than offense. Our country cannot survive and defend itself on some far-distant battlefield if our economic output is hampered by persistent cyberattack. Our politicians will not be able to gather public support to fight tyranny if fake news taints the opinions of the electorate. These are real issues we face today that will only get worse with time if we do not address them now.

Perhaps the first place to start is by addressing problems with the government's vulnerability equities process (VEP). The VEP is "an internal framework for determining when and whether the US government should publicly disclose newly-discovered software and hardware vulnerabilities."[191] Essentially, it is a mechanism for intelligence and law-enforcement agencies to disclose the top-secret list of software vulnerabilities that are used to spy. These software bugs are not known to the general public but might also be known to malicious hackers and other countries' intelligence services.

The current VEP process is broken because it allows federal agencies too much discretion on whether to release any vulnerabilities from their secret trove. Most intelligence and law-enforcement agencies choose to "stockpile, and utilize vulnerabilities for as long as possible and to disclose as infrequently as possible."[192] Releasing previously unknown vulnerabilities through VEP gives technology companies the ability to address their flawed products before other hackers discover the vulnerability too. In essence, our intelligence and law-enforcement agencies are making a flawed choice that offensive operations are more important than operations designed to protect US citizens and the business community.

The 2013 "Report and Recommendations of the President's Review Group on Intelligence and Communications Technologies" proposed a change to VEP to allow use of newly discovered vulnerabilities by the intelligence community in "rare instances" and under strict circumstances. Instead, the report recommends the focus should be on fixing and patching vulnerabilities.[193] Further, many in the security community believe that "the government's process should continue to be biased towards disclosure, and retention of vulnerabilities for government use should be permissible in defined circumstances."[194]

The PATCH Act, recently introduced legislation, would remove the White House and National Security Council from making decisions surrounding VEP. Instead, it creates a panel led by the Department of Homeland Security focused on "swiftly balancing the need to disclose vulnerabilities with other national security interests while increasing transparency and accountability to maintain public trust in the process," essentially giving defensive-friendly vulnerability disclosures the priority.[195]

Additionally, the government recently issued a revised charter for the VEP program, creating more transparency into the process.[196] Unfortunately, the evaluation and disclosure process is still run by US intelligence agencies that have had a spotty record of disclosing vulnerabilities in the past.

Notifying vendors of vulnerabilities will give them the opportunity to create software fixes that can be installed by those who use the software. This helps reduce the number of software holes hackers can use to attack.

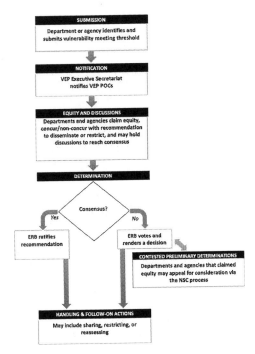

Vulnerabilities Equity Process[197]

VEP reform is a vital bridge, giving private industry time to improve address software. Increasing the number of VEP disclosures will improve security within the technology community. VEP improvements might serve as a bridge while the software industry figures out how to fix software bugs before they are ever released to the public.

While changing government norms that drive poor cybersecurity is critical, we also need to change behavior; the government alone can't protect private industry from cybersecurity threats. Corporate boards and senior leaders have an important role to play, and they are failing their employees and shareholders.

XII

Corporate Governance

Senior corporate leaders and boards of directors play a critical role in promoting cybersecurity programs within their companies. First and foremost, they are critical stakeholders and risk owners who are ultimately accountable for outlining strategy and establishing oversight. Unfortunately, most corporate boards and senior corporate leaders fail to align their cybersecurity programs with the strategic objectives of their company; this does a huge disservice to shareholders and customers.[198]

CEOs often fail to "come to grips with the fact that they are managing digital businesses that are under attack," pushing cybersecurity and data protection far from the top of the corporate priority list.[199] Increasingly, CEOs are being held accountable for this failure. The CEOs of Target and Equifax were fired over their companies' inadequate ability to detect and respond to breaches.

Corporate boards are failing too. Boards have oversight responsibilities and are responsible for making sure major corporate risks are addressed. Many still have not incorporated appropriate oversight and governance around their corporate cybersecurity programs. The big challenge for many boards is that cybersecurity is relatively foreign and potentially anathema to business leaders globally. The new reality is that cybersecurity presents critical business challenges that are well suited for boardroom discussions.[200] Changing attitudes in the C-suite and with boards of directors will be key to improving cybersecurity in the private sector.

The National Association of Corporate Directors (NACD), a global organization of more than seventeen thousand boards of directors, recommends its members focus on several key principles to ensure cybersecurity risk is managed appropriately. The NACD promotes the notion that "cybersecurity is an enterprise-wide risk management issue, not just an IT issue."[201] They also recommend corporate boards clearly understand the legal cyber risk implications for their company's industry; ensure they have adequate access to cybersecurity expertise; make sure cyber risk-management programs are developed, staffed, and funded; and recognize their own oversight responsibilities, giving adequate time to program reviews on their board agendas.[202]

While boards and senior corporate leaders are taking more steps to understand and manage cyber risk, they are often given an incomplete picture of a company's risk landscape; this hampers their ability to manage cyber risk.

In an effort to establish routine board governance guidelines I developed the G4 Cybersecurity Board Governance Model. The model seeks to simplify the complexities of risk-management reporting by recommending boards focus on four key elements in assessing the adequacy of their companies' cybersecurity programs. G4 recommends asking four key questions as the basis for cybersecurity governance and oversight: "How well does your company assess risk, protect itself from attacks, detect intrusions and manage legal IT compliance gaps?"[203]

Of course, as with every governance framework, the devil is in the details. So G4 maps each of these four questions back to expansive governance models such as the NIST Cybersecurity Framework, ISO 27001, and a series of other globally respected cybersecurity frameworks.

G4 also recommends boards commission outside experts to help validate management assertions about the effectiveness of its response to its four questions, along with its overall cybersecurity strategy.[204] The goal of G4 is to help boards simplify complex cyber requirements into a few simple, digestible business objectives while creating an environment of accountability and promoting a continuous-improvement process in cybersecurity risk.[205] Regardless of the model used, corporate boards and senior leaders should promote several key principles as part of a healthy cybersecurity program.

Cybersecurity risk-management programs begin with a fundamental understanding of what you are protecting (asset management), how it needs to be protected (governance), how your business environment contributes to risk, what your most concerning risks are, and how you plan to address them.

We know from previous chapters that managing cyber risk is challenging because most companies operate within a complex technical ecosystem, and many risks are outside their control or field of vision. But the true reality is many companies fail to adequately understand cybersecurity risk at the highest levels of management. This often leaves risk-management decisions in the hands of middle managers who may not be empowered to make the types of significant changes needed to reduce risk. So boards and senior managers need to know how good their companies are at assessing risks before they can begin to understand how proficient they are at addressing those risks.

Ensuring adequate technical, policy, and process controls in protecting a company's most prized assets and revenue streams is another critical component of the board's cybersecurity oversight. Understanding the types of detective and protective controls; the quality in which you maintain your assets; and your ability to assess changes in your environment, tune your protections, and train your personnel is key.

As we discussed in an earlier chapter, cybersecurity spending is up dramatically, but we also know cybersecurity programs are not yet adequately addressing cybersecurity challenges. Part of the gap may be due to the lack of effective detection and protection strategies that align people and processes with a company's technology investment. Failures to align all three often result in disastrous consequences. Anomalous behavior was detected during Target's breach, but the company failed to design the effective processes intended to streamline the company's ability to respond to active intrusions.[206] Understanding how well the company protects its assets is key to assessing how well you are addressing risk.

No matter how well you address and manage risk, there will always be a time when controls, technology, or people will fail. Adequate cybersecurity incident response and containment are often the final opportunities to address a threat before it leads to data loss or a general threat to a business's ability to operate.

The ability to detect anomalous behavior, respond, and recover from it are critical to a company's ability to contain direct attacks. As the chart below demonstrates, there are five critical phases to any successful data breach, and having the capabilities to detect and respond effectively at any stage will help reduce or even eliminate the impact of any breach.

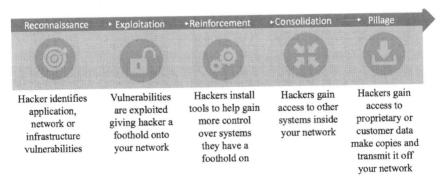

Reconnaissance	Exploitation	Reinforcement	Consolidation	Pillage
Hacker identifies application, network or infrastructure vulnerabilities	Vulnerabilities are exploited giving hacker a foothold onto your network	Hackers install tools to help gain more control over systems they have a foothold on	Hackers gain access to other systems inside your network	Hackers gain access to proprietary or customer data make copies and transmit it off your network

Phases of a Data Breach

Finally, there are so many different regulatory and sector-specific cybersecurity requirements facing companies today that it is often difficult for senior leaders and corporate boards to assess where regulatory gaps exist and ensure plans to address them are adequate. The failure for adequately addressing these gaps could be material. For example, the European General Data Protection Regulation, companies that insecurely store or process data on EU residents, could face stiff penalties of up to 4 percent of global revenue.[207]

	Governance (Maturity)	Metrics (Effectiveness)	Assessment (Independent Validation)
How well does your company manage IT risk?	Understanding Risk 1 2 3 4 5	Last Risk Assessment Goal: Q1 Actual: Q1	Risk Assessment Accuracy
	Risk Strategy Alignment 1 2 3 4 5	Unmanaged Risks Goal: <5% Actual: 18%	Unmanaged Risks Accuracy Last Performed: Q1 Results: Gaps
How well does your company protect its IT assets and data?	Identifying Breach Risk 1 2 3 4 5	Assets Vulnerable to Breach Goal: <5% Actual: 37%	Breach Assessment Accuracy
	Managing Protections 1 2 3 4 5	Protection Standards Met Goal: 95% Actual: 65%	Protection Standards Accuracy Last Performed: Q1 Results: Gaps
Can you protect the company against attacks?	Attack Detection 1 2 3 4 5	High Impact Incidents Goal: 0% Actual: 0%	Attack Detection Test
	Attack Containment 1 2 3 4 5		Attack Containment Test Last Performed: Q1 Results: Passed
Is the company meeting its IT compliance obligations?	Compliance Assessments 1 2 3 4 5	Last Assessment Goal: Q1 Actual: Q1	Compliance Gap Assessment Last Performed: Q1 Results: Accurate
	Compliance Management 1 2 3 4 5	Compliance Gaps Goal: <5% Actual: 20%	

G4 Cybersecurity Governance Model Dashboard Sample

Managing cybersecurity risk requires constant program evolution. Senior corporate leaders and corporate boards must demand cybersecurity programs that incorporate continuous-improvement principles. Today's programs will not typically address the advanced threats that will likely develop in the future unless they evolve.

Cybersecurity experts at Carnegie Mellon's Software Engineering Institute (SEI) recommend W. Edwards Deming's Plan, Do, Check, Act (PDCA) approach to continuous improvement. Deming believed this approach could be applied to any system, from an individual practice to a comprehensive program, to promote continuous improvement. SEI believes this is the perfect methodology for "security sustainment and improvement that can be applied to...a full-blown information security...management system."[208] Incorporating PDCA into a corporate governance model helps promote a comprehensive program that evolves over time.

Senior leaders and corporate boards should directly commission third parties to evaluate their cybersecurity programs. They must commission maturity and tactical assessments to make sure cybersecurity programs are managing risk and evolving effectively. Tracking maturity progression and effectiveness over time is key. So is evaluating the continual effectiveness of a program over time.

XIII

Where Do We Go from Here?

The moonshot solutions proposed in this book are a starting point. The book is meant to create a sense of urgency to promote a dialogue to fix cybersecurity.

We will need strong leadership in the public and private sectors to present a firm call to action and help develop a comprehensive strategy that will motivate others and drive momentum for our moonshot.

What we have learned from our study of moonshots in this book is that very difficult—even impossible—challenges can be solved if we put our minds, money, and collective efforts into finding solutions.

Right now, we don't have momentum, a consolidated strategy, or strong leadership—all of which are absolutely necessary to solve a problem on this scale. What we know is that time is not on our side. What we don't know is what the decisive "last straw" that will ultimately drive the momentum behind our moonshot will be.

Many talk about a future cyber Pearl Harbor that will wake leaders, stakeholders, and the public to the threat we're under and drive a comprehensive reckoning needed for our moonshot. Waiting for a cyber apocalypse to drive action is self-defeating and ill-advised.

Rather than wait, we must elevate the dialogue both inside and outside the cybersecurity community about acting *now* rather than later. We need enlightened leaders who have the ears of those in power to begin to help shift public opinion and address the norms behind the cyber conundrum. As mentioned earlier, time is not on our side, and there are a number of important technology developments that require us to act now.

Quantum computing promises to make new innovations possible by allowing us to leap dramatically beyond our current data-processing capabilities into the realms of science fiction. Encryption, antimalware, and a host of just about everything we rely on to secure our data and technology today will benefit and suffer from advances in quantum computing.

Add advances in artificial intelligence to advances in quantum computing, and you begin to see the challenge will become much greater in the future than the conundrum we struggle with today. Attacks can evolve and adjust without human interaction in ways and speeds that we cannot fathom today, but they will get only more intense, and defenses cybersecurity programs rely on today will become useless. Encryption as we know it will cease to shield our data from prying eyes. Malware and attacks will evolve at light speed, making detection and remediation difficult.

We know that managing cybersecurity risk in today's landscape is too complex for most companies to handle proficiently. A recent study found that "the average organization manages 55 security solutions ranging from endpoint security to infrastructure security and application security, and is spending $11.9 million per year responding to security incidents." [209]

Those costs will grow to unsustainable levels in the new world, where AI and quantum-computing threats dominate the landscape.

It is time to act. As we suggest in this book, software companies need to address security bugs before software is released to the general public. We need to educate corporate boards of directors, making sure they know how to drive the right risk-management outcomes. We need authentication platforms to evolve beyond passwords, to create more secure, human-friendly authentication technologies. We also need government leaders who aren't afraid to engage with technology companies to develop better long-term cybersecurity solutions and policy that evolves over time. The cyber conundrum is a national security issue that threatens our democracy and our prosperity.

There is likely no single strategy that will help us achieve our lofty moonshot ambitions. Legislation alone will not drive success. Competitive incentives alone will not be enough to drive innovation and make our moonshot successful. Altruism also will not get us there. It will take all of these forces to change the norms behind the cybersecurity challenges we struggle with today.

We have explored how FDR, Churchill, and Stalin led their people to victory in World War II. We touched on the lengths to which FDR and Basil O'Connor went to raise awareness and more than a billion dollars to fund research into preventing polio. We also touched the surface of Kennedy's influence on the space program and getting humans to the moon. Our moonshot needs leaders willing to stand up, draw a line in the sand, and issue the challenge to us all to secure our digital infrastructure, economy, and society.

We did not explore the millions of others who made our sample moonshots a reality by building planes, fighting battles, raising dimes, and computing course trajectories. Behind every moonshot is an army of dedicated tacticians who make the impossible possible. One thing we learned from our study of moonshots: people are willing to go so far as to risk their lives to achieve lofty objectives—but only if the objective is worthy. So no matter what we do, we need to make sure our strategy is clear so they can go about solving our cybersecurity moonshot the same way all moonshots are solved: with hard work, focused effort, and determination.

If we seize on this moment to adapt and change some of the fundamental norms driving today's state of insecurity, we may be able to leap beyond our own current limitations.

What we can say with some certainty is that if we don't try to solve this problem, it is not hard to see what is at stake. Trillions of dollars in losses from cybercrime or hybrid warfare are on the line. Our very democratic institutions are on the line, jeopardized by foreign propaganda designed to confuse our citizens and weaken hard-fought alliances. And if we don't evolve the way we protect the private and public sectors from cyber threats, America's very standing as a world leader may be at risk.

We must evolve into a world where cybersecurity challenges move from news headlines to footnotes in history books. Perhaps that vision is too ambitious, but isn't the goal of achieving the impossible the base ingredient in every successful moonshot?

Notes

Introduction

1. U*X*L American Decades. 2003. "The 1940s Science and Technology: Overview." Encyclopedia.com. Accessed November 12, 2017. http://www.encyclopedia.com/social-sciences/culture-magazines/1940s-science-and-technology-overview.

2. "Post–World War II Economic Expansion." 2017. Wikipedia. Last modified November 11. https://en.m.wikipedia.org/wiki/Post%E2%80%93World_War_II_economic_expansion.

3. Fallows, James. 2013. "The 50 Greatest Breakthroughs Since the Wheel." *The Atlantic*, November. https://www.theatlantic.com/magazine/archive/2013/11/innovations-list/309536/.

4. Shannon, C. E. 1948. "A Mathematical Theory of Communication." *The Bell System Technical Journal* 27 (3): 379–423. doi:10.1002/j.1538-7305.1948.tb01338.x.

5. "Claude Shannon." 2017. Wikipedia. Accessed November 12. https://en.m.wikipedia.org/wiki/Claude_Shannon.

6. Kahn, David. 1997. *The Codebreakers: The Comprehensive History of Secret Communication from Ancient Times to the Internet*. New York: Scribner's and Sons.

7. "Kerckhoffs's Principle." 2017. Wikipedia. Last modified November 4. https://en.m.wikipedia.org/wiki/Kerckhoffs%27s_principle.

Chapter 1

8. Timberg, Craig. 2015. "These Hackers Warned the Internet Would Become a Security Disaster. Nobody Listened."

Washington Post, June 22. http://www.washingtonpost. com/sf/business/2015/06/22/net-of-insecurity-part-3/?utm_ term=.3f24c96c7f2f.

9. Ibid.

10. Ibid.

11. Ibid.

12. Holt, John Matthew. 2017. "Oracle Is 'Patched' into a Software Crisis." SecurityInfoWatch.com. Accessed November 3. http:// www.securityinfowatch.com/article/12347921/oracle-is-patched-into-a-software-crisis.

13. Riley, Michael, and Dune Lawrence. 2014. "As Data Breach Woes Continue, Target's CEO Resigns." Bloomberg.com. Last modified May 5. https://www.bloomberg.com/news/articles/2014-05-05/as-data-breach-woes-continue-targets-ceo-resigns.

14. "Cybercrime Damage Costs $6 Trillion in 2021, Cybersecurity Market Data." 2016. Cybersecurity Ventures. Last modified August 12. http://cybersecurityventures.com/hackerpocalypse-cybercrime-report-2016/.

15. "Global Economic Crime Survey 2016." 2016. Pricewaterhouse Coopers. Accessed November 3, 2017. https://www.pwc.com/gx/en/services/advisory/forensics/economic-crime-survey. html.

16. Sheridan, Kelly. 2017. "Data Breaches Exposed 4.2 Billion Records In 2016." Dark Reading. Last modified January 25. http://www.

darkreading.com/attacks-breaches/data-breaches-exposed-42-billion-records-in-2016/d/d-id/1327976.

17. "Data Breaches." 2017. Privacy Rights Clearinghouse. Accessed November 3. https://www.privacyrights.org/data-breaches.

18. Ibid.

19. Ibid.

20. Menn, Joseph. 2017. "A Scramble at Cisco Exposes Uncomfortable Truths about US Cyber Defense." Reuters. Last modified March 30. http://www.reuters.com/article/us-usa-cyber-defense-idUSKBN17013U.

21. Olmstead, Kenneth, and Aaron Smith. 2017. "Americans and Cybersecurity." Pew Research Center: Internet, Science & Tech. Last modified January 25. http://www.pewinternet.org/2017/01/26/americans-and-cybersecurity/.

22. "Identity Theft Resource Center." 2017. ID Theft Center. Last modified January 19. http://www.idtheftcenter.org/2016data breaches.html.

23. Olmstead, Kenneth, and Aaron Smith. 2017. "Americans and Cybersecurity." Pew Research Center: Internet and Technology. Last modified January 25. http://www.pewinternet.org/2017/01/26/americans-and-cybersecurity/.

24. Timberg, Craig. 2015. "These Hackers Warned the Internet Would Become a Security Disaster. Nobody Listened." *Washington Post*, June 22. http://www.washingtonpost.com/sf/business/2015/06/22/net-of-insecurity-part-3/?utm_term=.3f24c96c7f2f.

25. "Global Economic Crime Survey 2016." 2017. PwC. Accessed November 3. https://www.pwc.com/gx/en/services/advisory/forensics/economic-crime-survey.html.

26. Morgan, Steve. 2016. "Worldwide Cybersecurity Spending Increasing to $170 Billion by 2020." *Forbes*, March 9. https://www.forbes.com/sites/stevemorgan/2016/03/09/worldwide-cybersecuity-spending-increasing-to-170-billion-by-2020/#68e478686832.

27. Associated Press. 2017. "Yahoo Punishes CEO Marissa Mayer over Hacks That Cost Firm $350 Million." *Telegraph*, March 2. http://www.telegraph.co.uk/technology/2017/03/02/yahoo-punishes-ceo-marissa-mayer-hacks-cost-firm-350-million/.

28. Spangler, Todd. 2017. "Yahoo CEO Marissa Mayer Loses Bonus, Top Lawyer Resigns in Wake of Massive Security Breaches." *Variety*, March 2. http://variety.com/2017/digital/news/yahoo-marissa-mayer-forego-bonus-stock-data-breaches-1202000240/.

29. "Cybersecurity in the Boardroom." 2017. NYSE Governance Series. Accessed November 3. http://www.nyse.com/public-docs/VERACODE_Survey_Report.pdf.

30. Olmstead, Kenneth, and Aaron Smith. 2017. "Americans and Cybersecurity." Pew Research Center: Internet and Technology. Last modified January 25. http://www.pewinternet.org/2017/01/26/americans-and-cybersecurity/.

31. Weedon, Jen, William Nuland, and Alex Stamos. 2017. "Information Operations and Facebook." Website Title. Accessed November 3. https://fbnewsroomus.files.wordpress.com/2017/04/facebook-and-information-operations-v1.pdf.

32. Wakabayashi, Mike, and Isaac Daisuke. 2017. "Russian Influence Reached 126 Million Through Facebook Alone." *New York Times*, October 30.

33. Maremont, Mark, and Rob Barry. 2017. "Russian Twitter Support for Trump Began Right After He Started Campaign." *Wall Street Journal*, November 6.

34. "United States Presidential Election, 2016." 2017. Wikipedia. Last modifiedNovember6.https://en.wikipedia.org/wiki/United_States_ presidential_election,_2016.

35. Ibid.

36. Pogue, David. 2017. "What Facebook Is Doing to Combat Fake News." *Scientific American*, February 1. https://www. scientificamerican.com/article/pogue-what-facebook- is-doing-to-combat-fake-news/.

37. Rossback, Neil, and Andrew Macfarquhar. 2017. "How Russian Propaganda Spread from a Parody Website to Fox News." *New York Times*, June 7. https://www.nytimes.com/interac- tive/2017/06/07/world/europe/anatomy-of-fake-news-russian- propaganda.html.

38. Rutenberg, Jim. 2017. "RT, Sputnik and Russia's New Theory of War." *New York Times*, September 13. https://www.nytimes. com/2017/09/13/magazine/rt-sputnik-and-russias-new-theory- of-war.html?_r.

39. Vitkovskaya, Julie, Samuel Granados, and John Muyskens. 2017. "The Post's New Findings in Russia's Bold Campaign to Influence the US Election." *Washington Post*, July 11. https://

www.washingtonpost.com/graphics/2017/world/national-security/russia-hacking-timeline/?utm_term=.a1e1068e0392.

Chapter 2

40. Daniel, Michael. 2017. "Why Is Cybersecurity So Hard?" *Harvard Business Review*, July 10. https://hbr.org/2017/05/why-is-cyber security-so-hard.

41. Onion, Rebecca. 2013. "How the Original Hackers Whistled Past Ma Bell's Security." *Slate*, February 1. http://www.slate.com/blogs/the_vault/2013/02/01/phone_phreaks_the_toy_whistles_early_hackers_used_to_break_into_the_phone.html.

42. "Source Lines of Code." 2017. Wikipedia. Last modified October 7. https://en.m.wikipedia.org/wiki/Source_lines_of_code.

43. "National Vulnerability Database." 2017. NVD—CVSS Severity Distribution Over Time. Accessed November 3. https://nvd.nist.gov/vuln-metrics/visualizations/cvss-severity-distribution-over-time.

44. Ibid.

45. Cohen, Tova. 2017. "Microsoft to Continue to Invest over $1 Billion a Year on Cyber Security." Reuters. Last modified January 26. http://www.reuters.com/article/us-tech-cyber-microsoft-idUSKBN15A1GA.

46. Vanian, Jonathan. 2016. "Here's How Much Businesses Worldwide Will Spend on Cybersecurity by 2020." *Fortune*, October 12. http://fortune.com/2016/10/12/cybersecurity-global-spending/.

47. "List of Countries by Military Expenditures." 2017. Wikipedia. Last modified October 29. https://en.m.wikipedia.org/wiki/List_of_countries_by_military_expenditures.

48. Gjelten, Tom. 2013. "Leaked Documents Reveal Budget Breakdown Between CIA, NSA." NPR. Last modified August 29. http://www.npr.org/templates/story/story.php?storyId=216924337.

Chapter 3

49. "World Bank Report on Poverty." 2017. The World Bank. Accessed November 3. http://data.worldbank.org/topic/poverty.

50. Cunningham, Aimee. 2017. "Global Access to Quality Health Care Has Improved in the Last Two Decades." *Science News*, June 13. https://www.sciencenews.org/article/global-access-quality-health-care-has-improved-last-two-decades.

51. Washington, Nicole. 2016. "Billions of People Got Clean Water in the Past 25 Years." *National Geographic*, March 2. http://news.nationalgeographic.com/2016/03/160301-global-potable-water-access-graphic-data-points/.

52. "List of Countries by Life Expectancy." 2017. Wikipedia. Last modified October 31. https://en.m.wikipedia.org/wiki/List_of_countries_by_life_expectancy.

53. "Household Expenditures and Income." 2016. The Pew Charitable Trusts. Last modified March 30. http://www.pewtrusts.org/en/research-and-analysis/issue-briefs/2016/03/household-expenditures-and-income.

54. Ibid.

55. Davey, Graham C. L. 2013. "What Do We Worry About?" *Psychology Today*, May 21. https://www.psychologytoday.com/blog/why-we-worry/201305/what-do-we-worry-about.

56. Fottrell, Quentin. 2017. "Half of American Families Are Living Paycheck to Paycheck." *MarketWatch*, April 30. http://www.marketwatch.com/story/half-of-americans-are-desperately-living-paycheck-to-paycheck-2017-04-04.

57. Keating, Raymond. 2016. "Gap Analysis #5: Americans' Lost Income." Small Business & Entrepreneurship Council. Last modified September 21. http://sbecouncil.org/2016/09/21/gap-analysis-5-americans-lost-income/.

58. "Household Expenditures and Income." 2016. The Pew Charitable Trusts. Last modified March 30. http://www.pewtrusts.org/en/research-and-analysis/issue-briefs/2016/03/household-expenditures-and-income.

59. McKendrick, Joe. 2015. "Digital Technologies Will Soon Add $1 Trillion-Plus to Global Economy." *Forbes*, June 18. https://www.forbes.com/sites/joemckendrick/2015/03/17/digital-technologies-will-soon-add-1-trillion-plus-to-global-economy/#2e6389c521b8.

60. Gompert, David, and Hans Binnendijk. 2016. *The Power to Coerce*. Google Books. https://tinyurl.com/y88jexe8.

61. Greenberg, Andy. 2017. "How an Entire Nation Became Russia's Test Lab for Cyberwar." *Wired*, June 19. https://www.wired.com/story/russian-hackers-attack-ukraine/.

62. Gross, Terry, and Andy Greenberg. 2017. "Experts Suspect Russia Is Using Ukraine as a Cyberwar Testing Ground." NPR. Last modified June 22. http://www.npr.org/2017/06/22/533951389/experts-suspect-russia-is-using-ukraine-as-a-cyberwar-testing-ground.

63. "Ukraine." 2017. The World Bank. Accessed November 3. http://data.worldbank.org/country/ukraine.

64. "Okun's Law." 2017. Wikipedia. Last modified October 8. https://en.wikipedia.org/wiki/Okun%27s_law.

65. "United States Labor Force Statistics—Seasonally Adjusted." 2017. Rhode Island Department of Labor and Training. Accessed November 3. http://www.dlt.ri.gov/lmi/laus/us/usadj.htm.

66. "Gross-Domestic-Product-(GDP)-by-Industry Data." 2017. US Department of Commerce Bureau of Economic Analysis. Accessed November 3. https://www.bea.gov/industry/gdpbyind_data.htm.

67. "United States Labor Force Statistics—Seasonally Adjusted." 2017. RI Department of Labor and Training. Accessed November 3. http://www.dlt.ri.gov/lmi/laus/us/usadj.htm.

68. Barnes, Michael, and Cieply Brooks. 2014. "Sony Cyberattack, First a Nuisance, Swiftly Grew Into a Firestorm." *New York Times*, December 30. https://www.nytimes.com/2014/12/31/business/media/sony-attack-first-a-nuisance-swiftly-grew-into-a-firestorm-.html.

69. McClean, Christopher. 2014. "5 Things the Sony Hack Exposed." CNBC. Last modified December 30. http://www.

cnbc.com/2014/12/30/5-things-the-sony-hack-exposed-commentary.html.

70. Agence France-Presse. 2014. "Hack Attack Causes 'Massive Damage' at Steel Works." BBC News. Last modified December 22. http://www.bbc.com/news/technology-30575104.

71. Ibid.

Chapter 4

72. Levine, Michael. 2012. "Logic and Emotion," *Psychology Today*, July 12. https://www.psychologytoday.com/blog/the-divided-mind/201207/logic-and-emotion.

73. Casadevall, Arturo, and Ferric Fang. 2016. "Moonshot Science—Risks and Benefits." *mBio* 7 (4). doi: 10.1128/mBio.01381-16.

74. Fischer, Andreas, Samuel Greif, and Joachim Funke. 2012. "The Process of Solving Complex Problems," Master's Thesis. *The Journal of Problem Solving* 4, (1): 19–42. http://docs.lib.purdue.edu/cgi/viewcontent.cgi?article=1118&context=jps.

75. Young, H. Peyton. 2016. "Social Norms and Public Policy." Brookings. Last modified July 28. https://www.brookings.edu/research/social-norms-and-public-policy/.

Chapter 5

76. Gunn, Eileen. 2014. "How America's Leading Science Fiction Authors Are Shaping Your Future." Smithsonian.com. Last

modified May 1. http://www.smithsonianmag.com/arts-culture/ how-americas-leading-science-fiction-authors-are-shaping-your-future-180951169/#spOUMI1AZ2S80bwl.99.

77. "From the Earth to the Moon." 2017. Wikipedia. Accessed November 3. https://en.m.wikipedia.org/wiki/From_the_Earth_to_the_Moon# Influence_on_popular_culture.

78. Kennedy, John F. 1961. "The Decision to Go to the Moon: President John F. Kennedy's May 25, 1961 Speech before a Joint Session of Congress." NASA. Last modified October 29, 2013. https://history.nasa.gov/moondec.html.

79. "This Day in History: JFK Asks Congress to Support the Space Program." 2017. History.com. Accessed November 3. http://www. history.com/this-day-in-history/jfk-asks-congress-to-support-the-space-program.

80. Kennedy, John F. 1961. "The Decision to Go to the Moon: President John F. Kennedy's May 25, 1961 Speech before a Joint Session of Congress." NASA. Last modified October 29, 2013. https://history.nasa.gov/moondec.html.81.

81. Segal, Gerald. 1987. *The Simon & Schuster Guide to the World Today*. New York: Simon & Schuster.

82. Bacon, Edwin, and Mark Sandle. 2003. "Brezhnev Reconsidered." *Studies in Russian and East European History and Society*.

83. Tuff, Bansi, and Geoff Nagji. 2014. "A Simple Tool You Need to Manage Innovation." *Harvard Business Review*, July 23. https:// hbr.org/2012/05/a-simple-tool-you-need-to-mana.

84. "The Dawn of the Space Age." 2013. Central Intelligence Agency. Last modified February 5. https://www.cia.gov/news-information/featured-story-archive/2007-featured-story-archive/the-dawn-of-the-space-age.html.

85. Isserman, Maurice, and Michael Kazin. "America Divided: The Civil War of the 1960s." *New York Times*. Accessed November 3, 2017. http://www.nytimes.com/books/first/i/isserman-divided.html.

86. Kennedy, John F. 1961. "The Decision to Go to the Moon: President John F. Kennedy's May 25, 1961 Speech before a Joint Session of Congress." NASA. Last modified October 29, 2013. https://history.nasa.gov/moondec.html.

87. Dunbar, Brian. "Project Mercury Goals." NASA. Accessed November 3, 2017. https://www.nasa.gov/mission_pages/mercury/missions/goals.html.

88. Loff, Sarah. 2015. "Gemini—Bridge to the Moon." NASA. Last modified February 23. https://www.nasa.gov/mission_pages/gemini/index.html.

89. "Project Gemini." 2017. Wikipedia. Last modified October 27. https://en.m.wikipedia.org/wiki/Project_Gemini.

90. Loff, Sarah. 2015. "The Apollo Missions." NASA. Last modified March 16. https://www.nasa.gov/mission_pages/apollo/missions/index.html.

91. Schwindt, Oriana. 2017. "This Astronaut Found Sunken Treasure from Space and Kept It Secret until His Deathbed." VICE News. Accessed November 3. https://news.vice.com/story/this-astronaut-

found-sunken-treasure-from-space-and-kept-it-secret-until-his-deathbed.

92. Ibid.

93. Riley, Christopher. 2012. "Apollo 40 Years On: How the Moon Missions Changed the World Forever." *Observer*, December 15. https://www.theguardian.com/science/2012/dec/16/apollo-legacy-moon-space-riley.

Chapter 6

94. Horne, John. 2002. "Introduction." In *State, Society and Mobilization in Europe during the First World War.* Cambridge: Cambridge University Press, 237–39.

95. Paxton, Robert O. 2005. *The Anatomy of Fascism*. New York: Vintage Books, 103.

96. Ibid., 104.

97. Ibid., 106.

98. Ibid.

99. Freedland, Jonathan. 2017. "The 1930s Were Humanity's Darkest, Bloodiest Hour. Are You Paying Attention?" *Guardian*, March 11. https://www.theguardian.com/society/2017/mar/11/1930s-humanity-darkest-bloodiest-hour-paying-attention-second-world-war.

100. "World War II Casualties." 2017. Wikipedia. Last modified October 29. https://en.wikipedia.org/wiki/World_War_II_casualties.

101. Ebner, Michael. 2017. "How Fascists Took Over Italy with Widespread, Intensely Personal Acts of Political Violence." *Slate*, January 30. http://www.slate.com/articles/news_and_politics/fascism/2017/01/how_italian_fascists_succeeded_in_taking_over_italy.html.

102. Chow, Brian, and Stefen Mockenhaupt. 2016. "The Most Treacherous Battle of World War I Took Place in the Italian Mountains." Smithsonian.com. Last modified June 1. http://www.smithsonianmag.com/history/most-treacherous-battle-world-war-i-italian-mountains-180959076/.

103. "List of Countries by Population in 1939." 2017. Wikipedia. Last modified October 30. https://en.wikipedia.org/wiki/List_of_countries_by_population_in_1939.

104. "Unemployment Statistics during the Great Depression." 2017. United States History. Accessed November 3. http://www.u-s-history.com/pages/h1528.html.

105. Calamur, Krishnadev. 2017. "A Short History of 'America First.'" *The Atlantic*, January 21. https://www.theatlantic.com/politics/archive/2017/01/trump-america-first/514037/.

106. "Imperial Japanese Army." 2017. Wikipedia. Last modified October 17. https://en.wikipedia.org/wiki/Imperial_Japanese_Army.

107. "Royal Italian Army during World War II." 2017. Wikipedia. Last modified October 26. https://en.wikipedia.org/wiki/Royal_Italian_Army_during_World_War_II.

108. Harrison, Mark. 2000. *The Economics of World War II: Six Great Powers in International Comparison.* Cambridge: Cambridge University Press, 1–42.

109. Roosevelt, Franklin Delano. 1940. "Address of the President: University of Virginia." FDR Library. Accessed Month Day, 2017. http://www.fdrlibrary.marist.edu/_resources/images/msf/msf01330.

110. Taylor, Alan. 2011. "World War II: Operation Barbarossa." *The Atlantic*, July 24. https://www.theatlantic.com/photo/2011/07/world-war-ii-operation-barbarossa/100112/.

111. Overy, Richard. 2011. "History—World Wars: World War Two: How the Allies Won." BBC. Last modified February 17. http://www.bbc.co.uk/history/worldwars/wwtwo/how_the_allies_won_01.shtml.

112. Ibid.

113. Taylor, Alan. 2011. "World War II: Operation Barbarossa." *The Atlantic*, July 24. https://www.theatlantic.com/photo/2011/07/world-war-ii-operation-barbarossa/100112/.

114. "Military Production during World War II." 2017. Wikipedia. October 29. https://en.wikipedia.org/wiki/Military_production_during_World_War_II.

115. Burns, Ken. 2017. "The War." PBS. Accessed November 3. http://www.pbs.org/thewar/at_home_war_production.htm.

116. Ibid.

117. "Military Production during World War II." 2017. Wikipedia. Last modified October 29. https://en.wikipedia.org/wiki/ Military_production_during_World_War_II.

118. Beauchamp, Scott. 2016. "America's Misplaced Faith in Bombing Campaigns." *The Atlantic*, January 30. https://www.theatlantic. com/politics/archive/2016/01/bombs-away/433845/.

119. Ibid.

120. Wilson Ward. 2016. "The Bomb Didn't Beat Japan...Stalin Did." Foreign Policy. Last modified May 31. http://foreignpol- icy.com/2013/05/30/the-bomb-didnt-beat-japan-stalin-did/.

121. Overy, Richard. 2011. "History—World Wars: World War Two: How the Allies Won." BBC. Last modified February 17. http:// www.bbc.co.uk/history/worldwars/wwtwo/how_the_allies_ won_01.shtml.

122. "World War II Casualties." 2017. Wikipedia. Last modified October 29. https://en.wikipedia.org/wiki/World_War_II_casualties.

Chapter 7

123. "Roosevelt's Little White House at Warm Springs—Presidents: A Discover Our Shared Heritage Travel Itinerary." 2017. National Parks Service. Accessed November 3. https://www. nps.gov/nr/travel/presidents/roosevelts_little_white_house. html.

124. Klein, Christopher. 2014. "8 Things You May Not Know About Jonas Salk and the Polio Vaccine." History.com. Last modified

October 28. http://www.history.com/news/8-things-you-may-not-know-about-jonas-salk-and-the-polio-vaccine.

125. "Poliomyelitis (polio)." 2017. World Health Organization. Accessed November 3. http://www.who.int/topics/poliomyelitis/en/.

126. Beaubien, Jason. 2012. "Wiping Out Polio: How the US Snuffed Out a Killer." NPR. Last modified October 15. http://www.npr.org/sections/health-shots/2012/10/16/162670836/wiping-out-polio-how-the-u-s-snuffed-out-a-killer.

127. Ibid.

128. Ibid.

129. The College of Physicians of Philadelphia. 2017. "Timeline." The History of Vaccines. Accessed November 3. https://www.historyofvaccines.org/timeline.

130. The College of Physicians of Philadelphia. 2017. "Vaccine Development, Testing, and Regulation." The History of Vaccines. Accessed November 3. https://www.historyofvaccines.org/content/articles/vaccine-development-testing-and-regulation.

131. Lilienfeld, D. E. 2008. "The First Pharmacoepidemiologic Investigations: National Drug Safety Policy in the United States, 1901–1902." *Perspectives in Biology and Medicine*, 51 (2). https://www.ncbi.nlm.nih.gov/pubmed/18453724.

132. "This Day in History: Jenner Tests Smallpox Vaccine." 2017. History.com. Accessed November 3. http://www.history.com/this-day-in-history/jenner-tests-smallpox-vaccine.

133. "About Jonas Salk." 2017. Salk Institute for Biological Studies. Accessed November 3. http://www.salk.edu/about/history-of-salk/jonas-salk/.

134. "Jonas Salk." 2017. Biography.com. Last modified April 28. https://www.biography.com/people/jonas-salk-9470147.

135. "About Jonas Salk." 2017. Salk Institute for Biological Studies. Accessed November 3. http://www.salk.edu/about/history-of-salk/jonas-salk/.

136. "Whatever Happened to Polio?" 2005. National Museum of American History. Last modified February 1. http://amhistory. si.edu/polio/virusvaccine/vacraces2.htm.

137. Beaubien, Jason. 2012. "Wiping Out Polio: How the US Snuffed Out a Killer." NPR. Last modified October 15. http://www.npr.org/sections/health-shots/2012/10/16/162670836/wiping-out-polio-how-the-u-s-snuffed-out-a-killer.

138. Klein, Christopher. 2014. "8 Things You May Not Know About Jonas Salk and the Polio Vaccine." History.com. Last modified October 28. http://www.history.com/news/8-things-you-may-not-know-about-jonas-salk-and-the-polio-vaccine.

139. The College of Physicians of Philadelphia. 2017. "Timeline." The History of Vaccines. Accessed November 3. https://www. historyofvaccines.org/timeline.

140. "Polio Cases, Deaths, and Vaccination Rates—Vaccines—ProCon.org." 2017. ProConorg Headlines. Accessed November 25. https://vaccines.procon.org/view.additional-resource.php?resourceID=005964.

141. Beaubien, Jason. 2012. "Wiping Out Polio: How the US Snuffed Out a Killer." NPR. Last modified October 15. http://www.npr.org/sections/health-shots/2012/10/16/162670836/wiping-out-polio-how-the-u-s-snuffed-out-a-killer.

142. Whitman, Alden. 1972. "Basil O'Connor, Polio Crusader, Dies." *New York Times*, March 10. http://www.nytimes.com/1972/03/10/archives/basil-oconnor-polio-crusader-dies.html.

143. Ibid.

144. Ibid.

Chapter 8

145. "2017 DBIR: Understand Your Cybersecurity Threats." 2017. Verizon Enterprise Solutions. Last modified May 2. http://www.verizonenterprise.com/verizon-insights-lab/dbir/2017/.

146. Filkins, Barbara. 2016. "Information Security Spending Trends." SANS Institute. Last modified February. https://www.sans.org/reading-room/whitepapers/analyst/security-spending-trends-36697+.

147. "List of the Largest Information Technology Companies." 2017. Wikipedia. Accessed November 3. https://en.m.wikipedia.org/wiki/List_of_the_largest_information_technology_companies.

148. Shaban, Hamza. 2017. "Google Spent the Most It Ever Has Trying to Influence Washington: $6 Million." *Washington Post*, July 21. https://www.washingtonpost.com/news/the-switch/wp/2017/07/21/google-spent-the-most-it-ever-

has-trying-to-influence-washington-6-million/?utm_
term=.%2B011d310743ee.

149. Lunden, Ingrid. 2015. "6.1B Smartphone Users Globally by 2020, Overtaking Basic Fixed Phone Subscriptions." TechCrunch. Last modified June 2. https://techcrunch.com/2015/06/02/6-1b-smartphone-users-globally-by-2020-overtaking-basic-fixed-phone-subscriptions/.

150. Lunden, Ingrid. 2012. "Forrester: 760M Tablets in Use by 2016, Apple 'Clear Leader', Frames Also Enter the Frame." TechCrunch. Last modified April 24. https://techcrunch.com/2012/04/24/forrester-760m-tablets-in-use-by-2016-apple-clear-leader-frames-also-enter-the-frame/.

Chapter 9

151. Cohen, Tova. 2017. "Microsoft to Continue to Invest over $1 Billion a Year on Cyber Security." Reuters. Last modified January 26. https://www.reuters.com/article/us-tech-cyber-microsoft/microsoft-to-continue-to-invest-over-1-billion-a-year-on-cyber-security-idUSKBN15A1GA.

152. Lipner, Steve. 2017. "The Trustworthy Computing Security Development Lifecycle." Advanced Computer Security Applications Conference. Accessed November 3. https://www.acsac.org/2004/papers/Lipner.pdf.

153. "Top 50 Vendors by Total Number of 'Distinct' Vulnerabilities." 2017. CVE Details. Accessed November 3. https://www.cvedetails.com/top-50-vendors.php?year=0.

154. "OWASP Top Ten Project." 2017. OWASP. Accessed November 3. https://www.owasp.org/index.php/Category:OWASP_Top_Ten_Project#tab=OWASP_Top_10_for_2017_Release_Candidate_1.

155. "By the Numbers." 2016. Underwriters Laboratories. Last modified April 4. http://www.ul.com/aboutul/what-we-do/by-the-numbers/.

156. Meier, Barry. 1991. "What the U.L. Seal of Approval Signifies: A Case in Point." New York Times, March 22. http://www.nytimes.com/1991/03/23/news/what-the-ul-seal-of-approval-signifies-a-case-in-point.html?pagewanted=all.

157. Chirgwin, Richard. 2015. "Former L0pht Man 'Mudge' Leaves Google for Washington." The Register, July 1. https://www.theregister.co.uk/2015/07/01/mudge_leaves_chocolate_factory_for_washington/.

158. Knake, Robert. 2015. "Q&A With Peiter Zatko (aka Mudge): Setting Up the Cyber Independent Testing Laboratory." Council on Foreign Relations. Last modified December 18. https://www.cfr.org/blog/qa-peiter-zatko-aka-mudge-setting-cyber-independent-testing-laboratory.

159. "Top Teams' Automated Cybersecurity Systems Preparing for Final Face-Off." 2016. Defense Advanced Research Projects Agency. Last modified July 13. https://www.darpa.mil/news-events/2016-07-13.

160. "Mayhem Declared Preliminary Winner of Historic Cyber Grand Challenge." 2014. Defense Advanced Research Projects

Agency. Last modified August 4. https://www.darpa.mil/news-events/2016-08-04.

161. Press, Gil. 2017. "Top 10 Hot Artificial Intelligence (AI) Technologies." *Forbes*, March 29. https://www.forbes.com/sites/gilpress/2017/01/23/top-10-hot-artificial-intelligence-ai-technologies/#712a9c9f1928.

Chapter 10

162. Mathews, Lee. 2017. "Phishing Scams Cost American Businesses Half a Billion Dollars a Year." *Forbes*, May 5. https://www.forbes.com/sites/leemathews/2017/05/05/phishing-scams-cost-american-businesses-half-a-billion-dollars-a-year/#4aa3f2933fa1.

163. Kerravala, Zeus. 2017. "How AI Can Stop Tomorrow's Malware Threats Today." CSO Online. Last modified October 11. https://www.csoonline.com/article/3232448/network-security/how-ai-can-stop-tomorrows-malware-threats-today.html.

164. Herley, Cormac, and Paul Van Oorschot. 2011. "A Research Agenda Acknowledging the Persistence of Passwords." Microsoft.com. Last modified August 25. https://tinyurl.com/yc4293nz.

165. Le Bras, Tom. 2015. "Online Overload—It's Worse than You Thought." Dashlane Blog. Last modified July 21. https://blog.dashlane.com/infographic-online-overload-its-worse-than-you-thought/.

166. Vigliarolo, Brandon. 2016. "LastPass: The Smart Person's Guide." TechRepublic. Last modified November 9. https://www.techrepublic.com/article/lastpass-the-smart-persons-guide/.

167. Gibbs, Samuel. 2016. "Dropbox Hack Leads to Leaking of 68m User Passwords on the Internet." *The Guardian*, August 31. https://www.theguardian.com/technology/2016/aug/31/dropbox-hack-passwords-68m-data-breach.

168. Olmstead, Kenneth, and Aaron Smith. 2017. "Americans and Cybersecurity." Pew Research Center: Internet and Technology. Last modified January 25. http://www.pewinternet.org/2017/01/26/americans-and-cybersecurity/.

169. Gibbs, Samuel. 2016. "Dropbox Hack Leads to Leaking of 68m User Passwords on the Internet." *The Guardian*, August 31. https://www.theguardian.com/technology/2016/aug/31/dropbox-hack-passwords-68m-data-breach.

170. Segal Bernard, Tara, and Stacy Cowley. 2017. "Equifax Breach Caused by Lone Employee's Error, Former CEO Says." *New York Times*, October 3. https://www.nytimes.com/2017/10/03/business/equifax-congress-data-breach.html?_r=0.

171. Demos, Telis, and Peter Rudegeair. 2017. "Social Security Numbers: Hacked, Hated—and Irreplaceable." *Wall Street Journal*, October 16. https://www.wsj.com/articles/social-security-numbers-hacked-hatedand-irreplaceable-1508146202.

172. Gibbs, Samuel. 2016. "SS7 Hack Explained: What Can You Do about It?" *The Guardian*, April 19. https://www.theguardian.com/technology/2016/apr/19/ss7-hack-explained-mobile-phone-vulnerability-snooping-texts-calls.

173. "Nokia Threat Intelligence Report." 2017. Nokia. Accessed November 3. https://resources.ext.nokia.com/asset/201094+.

174. Sakimura, Nat. 2013. "Identity, Authentication + OAuth = OpenID Connect." YouTube. Last modified June 26. https://www.youtube.com/watch?v=Kb56GzQ2pSk&app=desktop.

175. Perez, Sarah. 2016. "Google Plans to Bring Password-Free Logins to Android Apps by Year-End." TechCrunch. Last modified May 23. https://techcrunch.com/2016/05/23/google-plans-to-bring-password-free-logins-to-android-apps-by-year-end/.

176. Chandra, Deepak. 2015. "Google I O 2015 Project Abacus ATAP." YouTube. Last modified May 29. https://www.youtube.com/watch?v=IGrRYnqHegc.

Chapter 11

177. Bell, Peter. 2017. "Public Trust in Government: 1958–2017." Pew Research Center for the People and the Press. Last modified May 2. http://www.people-press.org/2017/05/03/public-trust-in-government-1958-2017/.

178. "Congress and the Public." 2017. Gallup.com. Accessed November 4. http://news.gallup.com/poll/1600/congress-public.aspx.

179. "Presidential Job Approval Center." 2017. Gallup.com. Accessed November 4. http://news.gallup.com/interactives/185273/presidential-job-approval-center.aspx?g_source=THE_PRESIDENCY&g_medium=topic&g_campaign=tiles.

180. Fingerhut, Hannah. 2015. "Beyond Distrust: How Americans View Their Government." Pew Research Center for the People and the Press. Last modified November 22. http://

www.people-press.org/2015/11/23/beyond-distrust-how-americans-view-their-government/.

181. "List of US Executive Branch Czars." 2017. Wikipedia. Accessed November 4, 2017. https://en.m.wikipedia.org/wiki/List_of_U.S._executive_branch_czars.

182. "Policy 'Czars' Are Vital, Problematic." 2009. *Forbes*, November 3. https://www.forbes.com/2009/11/02/policy-czar-administration-business-oxford.html.

183. Fletcher, Michael. 2009. "Obama Critics Say Policy 'Czars' Skirt Proper Oversight, Vetting." *Washington Post*, September 16. http://www.washingtonpost.com/wp-dyn/content/article/2009/09/15/AR2009091501424.html.

184. James, Randy. 2009. "White House Czars: A Brief History." *Time*, September 23. http://time.com/3516927/history-of-white-house-czars/.

185. Young, H. Peyton. 2016. "Social Norms and Public Policy." Brookings. Last modified July 28. https://www.brookings.edu/research/social-norms-and-public-policy/.

186. Ibid.

187. "Economic Instruments as a Lever for Policy." 2017. WHO. Accessed November 4. http://www.who.int/heli/economics/econinstruments/en/.

188. Ibid.

189. "Insurance 2020 & Beyond: Reaping the Dividends of Cyber Resilience." 2017. PricewaterhouseCoopers. Accessed November 4. https://www.pwc.com/gx/en/industries/financial-services/insurance/publications/insurance-2020-cyber.html.

190. Kohn, Alfie. 2014. "Why Incentive Plans Cannot Work." *Harvard Business Review*, August 1. https://hbr.org/1993/09/why-incentive-plans-cannot-work.

191. Aitel, David, and Matt Tait. 2016. "Everything You Know About the Vulnerability Equities Process Is Wrong." Lawfare. Last modified August 26. https://www.lawfareblog.com/everything-you-know-about-vulnerability-equities-process-wrong.

192. *Liberty and Security in a Changing World Report and Recommendations of the President's Review Group on Intelligence and Communications Technologies.* 2013. Washington, DC: White House.

193. Schwartz, Ari, and Robert Knake. 2016. "Government's Role in Vulnerability Disclosure: Creating a Permanent and Accountable Vulnerability Equities Process | Belfer Center for Science and International Affairs." Harvard Kennedy School Belfer Center for Science and International Affairs. Last modified June. https://www.belfercenter.org/publication/governments-role-vulnerability-disclosure-creating-permanent-and-accountable.

194. Ibid.

195. Olenick, Doug. 2017. "PATCH Act Introduced to Improve Federal Cybersecurity and Transparency." *SC Media US*, May 18. https://

www.scmagazine.com/patch-act-introduced-to-improve-federal-cybersecurity-and-transparency/article/662541.

196. "Vulnerabilities Equities Policy and Process for the United States Government." 2017. White House. Last modified November 15. https://www.whitehouse.gov/sites/whitehouse.gov/files/images/External%20-%20Unclassified%20VEP%20Charter%20FINAL.PDF.

197. Ibid.

Chapter 12

198. Cheng, J. Yo-Jud, and Boris Groysberg. 2017. "Why Boards Aren't Dealing with Cyberthreats." *Harvard Business Review*, September 21. https://hbr.org/2017/02/why-boards-arent-dealing-with-cyberthreats.

199. Chronis, Peter K. 2017. "G4 Cybersecurity Board Governance Model." G4 Model. Accessed November 4, 2017. https://www.g4model.com.

200. Ibid.

201. Krebs, Brian. 2015. "Inside Target Corp., Days After 2013 Breach." Krebs on Security (blog), September 21. https://krebsonsecurity.com/2015/09/inside-target-corp-days-after-2013-breach/.

202. "GDPR: Potential Fines for Data Security Breaches More Severe for Data Controllers than Processors." 2016. *The Register*, May 12. https://www.theregister.co.uk/2016/05/12/

gdpr_potential_fines_for_data_security_breaches_more_severe_for_data_controllers_than_processors_says_expert/.

203. Chronis, Peter K. 2017. "G4 Cybersecurity Board Governance Model." G4 Model. Accessed November 4, 2017. https://www.g4model.com.

204. Ibid.

205. Ibid.

206. Krebs, Brian. 2015. "Inside Target Corp., Days After 2013 Breach." Krebs on Security (blog), September 21. https://krebsonsecurity.com/2015/09/inside-target-corp-days-after-2013-breach/.

207. "GDPR: Potential Fines for Data Security Breaches More Severe for Data Controllers than Processors." 2016. *The Register*, May 12. https://www.theregister.co.uk/2016/05/12/gdpr_potential_fines_for_data_security_breaches_more_severe_for_data_controllers_than_processors_says_expert/.

208. Allen, Julia. 2006. "Plan, Do, Check, Act." Software Engineering Institute—Carnegie Mellon University. Last modified November.

Chapter 13

209. Castellanos, Sara. 2017. "Ex-NSA, FBI Officials Call for Cyber Cooperation Between Public and Private Sectors." *Wall Street Journal*, October 31. https://www.wsj.com/amp/articles/BL-CIOB-12976?responsive.

12105992R00072

Made in the USA
Lexington, KY
18 October 2018